D0559907

$\mathcal{T}$o

_____

$\mathcal{F}$ROM

_____

$\mathcal{M}$ESSAGE

_____

_____

_____

_____

Promises from God for Women

© 2003 Christian Art Gifts, RSA
Christian Art Gifts Inc., IL, USA

Compiled by Wilma Le Roux and Lynette Douglas
Designed by Christian Art Gifts

ISBN 1-86920-070-5

Printed in China

05 06 07 08 09 10 11 12 – 12 11 10 9 8 7 6

PROMISES
FROM GOD FOR
WOMEN

CONTENTS

$\mathcal{I}$NTRODUCTION

Blessed is the man who trusts in the LORD, And whose hope is the LORD.

Jeremiah 17:7, NKJV

The world bombards us with promises – promises of beauty, popularity, wealth, and fame. But most of the world's promises are empty – just glitzy advertising that fails to live up to its promises. And so we become cynical and feel that it might be "safer" to live without hope. Failure to live up to expectations – our own and other's – surrounds us on every side. And we wonder if there is anyone we can trust completely.

Then we turn to the Bible and find that it offers a higher hope: the ability to endure the difficult days we face, and the promise of a life filled with God's presence, now and forever. As we focus on the promises of God, we find a hope that sustains us, and a peace that passes all understanding. Because God is faithful to His Word even when we lose heart. Let the promises of God fill your heart with joy and your mouth with praise, today and always.

$\mathcal{A}$NGER

*Everyone should be quick to listen, slow to speak
and slow to become angry, for man's anger does not
bring about the righteous life that God desires.*

James 1:19-20, NIV

We so easily fail when it comes to one of
Jesus' most important commandments:
to love our neighbor. Loving the people
who love you isn't always all that easy, but
to wish those people who annoy you well
seems like too much to ask. No one likes
to come off second best, and usually we are
quite indignant when we do. Because we are
only human, we find it virtually impossible
to bless those who have persecuted us.

And yet the Lord asks it of us. Jesus was
willing to pray for and bless the people who
persecuted Him time and again. Even on
the cross He asked God to forgive His per-
secutors.

This is impossible if you are not a child
of God. It is only He who can enable you
to conquer your innate selfish nature and
to love and bless those people for whom
you feel no love.

How to handle

ANGER

But You are God, ready to pardon, gracious and merciful, slow to anger, abundant in kindness.

Nehemiah 9:17, NKJV

The LORD is merciful and gracious, slow to anger and abounding in steadfast love. He will not always chide, nor will he keep his anger forever.

Psalm 103:8-9, ESV

A wise man feareth, and departeth from evil: but the fool rageth, and is confident. He that is soon angry dealeth foolishly: and a man of wicked devices is hated.

Proverbs 14:16-17, KJV

Let all bitterness and wrath and anger and clamor and slander be put away from you, along with all malice.

Ephesians 4:31, ESV

But now you yourselves are to put off all these: anger, wrath, malice, blasphemy, filthy language out of your mouth.

Colossians 3:8, NKJV

For all the law is fulfilled in one word, even in this: "You shall love your neighbor as yourself." But if you bite and devour one another, beware lest you be consumed by one another!

Galatians 5:14-15, NKJV

A soft answer turneth away wrath: but grievous words stir up anger.

Proverbs 15:1, KJV

Do not be quickly provoked in your spirit, for anger resides in the lap of fools.

Ecclesiastes 7:9, NIV

Cease from anger, and forsake wrath: fret not thyself in any wise to do evil.

Psalm 37:8, KJV

Be angry and do not sin; do not let the sun go down on your anger, and give no opportunity to the devil.

Ephesians 4:26-27, ESV

A wrathful man stirreth up strife: but he that is slow to anger appeaseth strife.

Proverbs 15:18, KJV

It is better to dwell in the wilderness, than with a contentious and an angry woman.

Proverbs 21:19, KJV

He who is slow to anger is better than the mighty, and he who rules his spirit than he who takes a city.

Proverbs 16:32, NKJV

Surely the churning of milk bringeth forth butter, and the wringing of the nose bringeth forth blood: so the forcing of wrath bringeth forth strife.

Proverbs 30:33, KJV

For his anger lasts only a moment, but his favor lasts a lifetime; weeping may remain for a night, but rejoicing comes in the morning.

Psalm 30:5, NIV

Be angry, and do not sin.

Psalm 4:4, ESV

He who is slow to wrath has great understanding, but he who is impulsive exalts folly.

Proverbs 14:29, NKJV

ANXIETY

For He shall give His angels charge over you, to keep you in all your ways.

Psalm 91:11, NKJV

It would be naive to think that ominous clouds will not at some point gather, darkening our lives. It would be futile to try to ignore them in the foolish belief that, by denying their existence, they would eventually disappear. It is better to prepare for it by standing firm in a living faith in the almighty God who controls the storms.

However threatening the circumstances may be, it is imperative that you not allow anything to usurp God's pivotal role in your life. With Him as the center you will be able to maintain your balance at all times. When your entire being is consumed by reverence and love for God, you will discover that fear no longer rules your mind. Uncertainty is replaced by trust. The ominous clouds might still be present, but you will see the silver lining, and you will know that, behind every cloud, there is a loving Father who works all things for your good.

The Word's answer

to anxiety

Thus says the LORD, who created you, O Jacob, And He who formed you, O Israel: "Fear not, for I have redeemed you; I have called you by your name; You are Mine."

Isaiah 43:1, NKJV

"Peace I leave with you, my peace I give unto you: not as the world giveth, give I unto you. Let not your heart be troubled, neither let it be afraid."

John 14:27, KJV

There is no fear in love. But perfect love drives out fear, because fear has to do with punishment.

1 John 4:18, NIV

What then shall we say to these things? If God is for us, who can be against us?

Romans 8:31, ESV

The LORD is my light and my salvation; whom shall I fear? The LORD is the strength of my life; of whom shall I be afraid?

Psalm 27:1, NKJV

But whoso hearkeneth unto me shall dwell safely, and shall be quiet from fear of evil.

Proverbs 1:33, KJV

Commit thy way unto the LORD; trust also in him; and he shall bring it to pass.

Psalm 37:5, KJV

And the LORD, he it is that doth go before thee; he will be with thee, he will not fail thee, neither forsake thee: fear not, neither be dismayed.

Deuteronomy 31:8, KJV

When I am afraid, I put my trust in you. In God, whose word I praise, in God I trust; I shall not be afraid. What can flesh do to me?

Psalm 56:3-4, ESV

Be careful for nothing; but in every thing by prayer and supplication with thanksgiving let your requests be made known unto God. And the peace of God, which passeth all understanding, shall keep your hearts and minds through Christ Jesus.

Philippians 4:6-7, KJV

And we know that all things work together for good to those who love God, to those who are the called according to His purpose.

Romans 8:28, NKJV

Cast your burden on the LORD, and he will sustain you; he will never permit the righteous to be moved.

Psalm 55:22, ESV

For I am convinced that neither death nor life, neither angels nor demons, neither the present nor the future, nor any powers, neither height nor depth, nor anything else in all creation, will be able to separate us from the love of God that is in Christ Jesus our Lord.

Romans 8:38-39, NIV

Even though I walk through the valley of the shadow of death, I will fear no evil, for you are with me; your rod and your staff, they comfort me.

Psalm 23:4, NIV

*B*LESSING

*For you bless the righteous, O L*ord*; you cover him with favor as with a shield.*

Psalm 5:12, ESV

Many people are unaware of the immeasurable generosity of God. Their own needs and dire poverty blind them and separate them from the One who could ease their suffering and transform their poverty into luxury, if only they would obey Him. Scripture reveals to us that God is much more willing to give than we are to receive. If we would only pray and believe sincerely, we could receive that which we pray for. Many disciples want to believe unconditionally and yet there are few who want to utilize the key which God makes available to unlock His abundance.

If you bring a request to your heavenly Father, make sure you don't harbor doubt that He won't comply with your request. Such an attitude creates distrust, prayers are not answered until doubt is replaced by faith. God hears your prayers and will meet your every need from His treasure house – according to His glorious grace.

BIBLE

BLESSINGS

Blessed is the man who walks not in the counsel of the ungodly, nor stands in the path of sinners, nor sits in the seat of the scornful; but his delight is in the law of the LORD, and in His law he meditates day and night.

Psalm 1:1-2, NKJV

Blessed are all those who put their trust in Him.

Psalm 2:12, NKJV

Blessed is the one who finds wisdom, and the one who gets understanding, for the gain from her is better than gain from silver and her profit better than gold.

Proverbs 3:13-14, ESV

Blessed is he that considereth the poor: the LORD will deliver him in time of trouble.

Psalm 41:1, KJV

The LORD will give strength to His people; the LORD will bless His people with peace.

Psalm 29:11, NKJV

And I will make them and the places all around my hill a blessing, and I will send down the showers in their season; they shall be showers of blessing.

Ezekiel 34:26, ESV

He who despises his neighbor sins, but blessed is he who is kind to the needy.

Proverbs 14:21, NIV

"But I say to you who hear: Love your enemies, do good to those who hate you, bless those who curse you, and pray for those who spitefully use you."

Luke 6:27-28, NKJV

Bless those who persecute you; bless and do not curse.

Romans 12:14, NIV

Blessed is he whose transgression is forgiven, whose sin is covered. Blessed is the man unto whom the LORD imputeth not iniquity, and in whose spirit there is no guile.

Psalm 32:1-2, KJV

The blessing of the LORD, it maketh rich, and he addeth no sorrow with it.

Proverbs 10:22, KJV

Blessed is every one that feareth the LORD; that walketh in his ways. For thou shalt eat the labour of thine hands: happy shalt thou be, and it shall be well with thee. Behold, that thus shall the man be blessed that feareth the LORD.

Psalm 128:1-2, 4, KJV

O taste and see that the LORD is good: blessed is the man that trusteth in him.

Psalm 34:8, KJV

Now be pleased to bless the house of your servant, that it may continue forever in your sight; for you, O Sovereign LORD, have spoken, and with your blessing the house of your servant will be blessed forever.

2 Samuel 7:29, NIV

And blessed is she who believed that there would be a fulfillment of what was spoken to her from the Lord.

Luke 1:45, ESV

The LORD will open to you his good treasury, the heavens, to give the rain to your land in its season and to bless all the work of your hands.

Deuteronomy 28:12, ESV

COMPASSION

Be kind and compassionate to one another, forgiving each other, just as in Christ God forgave you.

Ephesians 4:32, NIV

Jesus provides us with an overview of how disciples should act. They should do good to others without expecting anything in return. It is much easier to do good to others if you know that they are going to reward you for your generosity. But Jesus wants you to be willing to lend without expecting to get anything back, to help those who are trying to harm you, and to reach out to others and provide for their needs without first trying to determine whether they deserve it. In short, you should do to others as you would have them do to you (see Lk. 6:31).

The reason is to be found in verse 36: *"Be merciful, just as your Father is merciful"* (NIV). Just think of how good God is to you, even though you don't deserve His grace at all. In the same way you need to be willing to do good to others who might not deserve it; to notice the distress of people around you and to do something about it.

THE COMPASSION
OF GOD

Trust in the LORD, and do good; so shalt
thou dwell in the land, and verily thou shalt
be fed.

Psalm 37:3, KJV

Do not forget to do good and to share, for
with such sacrifices God is well pleased.

Hebrews 13:16, NKJV

"A Samaritan, as he traveled, came where the
man was; and when he saw him, he took pity
on him. He went to him and bandaged his
wounds, pouring on oil and wine. Then he
put the man on his own donkey, took him
to an inn and took care of him. The next day
he took out two silver coins and gave them
to the innkeeper. 'Look after him,' he said,
'and when I return, I will reimburse you for
any extra expense you may have.'"

Luke 10:33-35, NIV

See that no one repays anyone evil for evil,
but always seek to do good to one another
and to everyone.

1 Thessalonians 5:15, ESV

As a father has compassion on his children, so the LORD has compassion on those who fear him.

Psalm 103:13, NIV

Learn to do well; seek judgment, relieve the oppressed, judge the fatherless, plead for the widow.

Isaiah 1:17, KJV

Suppose a brother or sister is without clothes and daily food. If one of you says to him, "Go, I wish you well; keep warm and well fed," but does nothing about his physical needs, what good is it?

James 2:15-16, NIV

But thou, O LORD, art a God full of compassion, and gracious, longsuffering, and plenteous in mercy and truth.

Psalm 86:15, KJV

Through the LORD's mercies we are not consumed, because His compassions fail not. Though He causes grief, yet He will show compassion according to the multitude of His mercies.

Lamentations 3:22, 32, NKJV

Unto the upright there ariseth light in the darkness: he is gracious, and full of compassion, and righteous.

Psalm 112:4, KJV

Therefore, as God's chosen people, holy and dearly loved, clothe yourselves with compassion, kindness, humility, gentleness and patience. Bear with each other and forgive whatever grievances you may have against one another.

Colossians 3:12-13, NIV

All of you be of one mind, having compassion for one another; love as brothers, be tender-hearted, be courteous; not returning evil for evil or reviling for reviling, but on the contrary blessing, knowing that you were called to this, that you may inherit a blessing.

1 Peter 3:8-9, NKJV

"Love your enemies, do good to them, and lend to them without expecting to get anything back. Be merciful, just as your Father is merciful."

Luke 6:35-36, NIV

CONFIDENCE

And this is the confidence that we have in him, that, if we ask any thing according to his will, he heareth us.

1 John 5:14, KJV

Confidence is not an art that many people have developed. You might rehearse what to say to your boss when requesting a raise, but when the time comes to speak up, you cannot find the words. You feel frustrated and a failure. A lack of confidence prevents you from attaining your full potential. You need to develop your ability to achieve success.

Fear, uncertainty, inferiority, fear of rejection could all contribute to your nervous attitude toward life. The only way to control these destructive influences is to take refuge in a greater influence that can overcome all these things and win your whole-hearted confidence. You meet this "greater influence" when you yield to Jesus Christ as the Lord of your life and you start living to love and serve Him. Then your confidence will grow by the day and you will start to lead a well-adjusted life.

THE WORD'S VIEW

ON CONFIDENCE

For who is God, save the LORD? and who is a rock, save our God? God is my strength and power: and he maketh my way perfect.

2 Samuel 22:32-33, KJV

Therefore do not cast away your confidence, which has great reward.

Hebrews 10:35, NKJV

Be not afraid of sudden fear, neither of the desolation of the wicked, when it cometh. For the LORD shall be thy confidence, and shall keep thy foot from being taken.

Proverbs 3:25-26, KJV

But Christ as a son over his own house; whose house are we, if we hold fast the confidence and the rejoicing of the hope firm unto the end.

Hebrews 3:6, KJV

Our gospel did not come to you in word only, but also in power, and in the Holy Spirit and in much assurance.

1 Thessalonians 1:5, NKJV

For we are made partakers of Christ, if we hold the beginning of our confidence stedfast unto the end.

Hebrews 3:14, KJV

And I am sure of this, that he who began a good work in you will bring it to completion at the day of Jesus Christ.

Philippians 1:6, ESV

In him and through faith in him we may approach God with freedom and confidence.

Ephesians 3:12, NIV

Let us then with confidence draw near to the throne of grace, that we may receive mercy and find grace to help in time of need.

Hebrews 4:16, ESV

So we are always confident, knowing that while we are at home in the body we are absent from the Lord. For we walk by faith, not by sight. We are confident, yes, well pleased rather to be absent from the body and to be present with the Lord.

2 Corinthians 5:6-8, NKJV

Jesus Christ the same yesterday, and to day, and for ever.

Hebrews 13:8, KJV

In the fear of the LORD is strong confidence: and his children shall have a place of refuge.

Proverbs 14:26, KJV

The fruit of righteousness will be peace; the effect of righteousness will be quietness and confidence forever.

Isaiah 32:17, NIV

Such is the confidence that we have through Christ toward God. Not that we are sufficient in ourselves to claim anything as coming from us, but our sufficiency is from God.

2 Corinthians 3:4-5, ESV

Beloved, if our heart does not condemn us, we have confidence toward God. And whatever we ask we receive from Him, because we keep His commandments and do those things that are pleasing in His sight.

1 John 3:21-22, NKJV

CONTENTMENT

My soul shall be satisfied as with marrow and fatness;
and my mouth shall praise thee with joyful lips.
Psalm 63:5, KJV

When our minds are stayed on the love and peace of God, we experience indescribable tranquillity and peace of mind.

When you set your mind on trusting God through every day and every sleepless night, calm and peace will descend upon your spirit. You will not only experience peace of mind, but you will also stop worrying about the well-being of your loved ones, because you have the assurance that they are safe in God's loving care.

By focusing on Jesus Christ and the peace and prosperity that He gives, you become calm and are set free because you know God is in control of your life. He leads you in paths of righteousness and there is no man or circumstance that can disturb your tranquillity. Then He sets you free from anxious worry and tension, because His love enfolds you.

Promises of
Contentment

Keep your life free from love of money, and be content with what you have, for he has said, "I will never leave you nor forsake you."

Hebrews 13:5, ESV

Godliness with contentment is great gain. For we brought nothing into the world, and we can take nothing out of it. But if we have food and clothing, we will be content with that.

1 Timothy 6:6-8, NIV

The fear of the LORD leads to life, and whoever has it rests satisfied; he will not be visited by harm.

Proverbs 19:23, ESV

I have learned in whatever state I am, to be content: I know how to be abased, and I know how to abound. Everywhere and in all things I have learned both to be full and to be hungry, both to abound and to suffer need. I can do all things through Christ who strengthens me.

Philippians 4:11-13, NKJV

For the sake of Christ, then, I am content with weaknesses, insults, hardships, persecutions, and calamities. For when I am weak, then I am strong.

2 Corinthians 12:10, ESV

If they obey and serve him, they will spend the rest of their days in prosperity and their years in contentment.

Job 36:11, NIV

"I will satiate the soul of the priests with abundance, and My people shall be satisfied with My goodness," says the LORD.

Jeremiah 31:14, NKJV

All the days of the afflicted are evil: but he that is of a merry heart hath a continual feast.

Proverbs 15:15, KJV

He satisfies the thirsty and fills the hungry with good things.

Psalm 107:9, NIV

Satisfy us in the morning with your steadfast love, that we may rejoice and be glad all our days.

Psalm 90:14, ESV

Be still, and know that I am God: I will be
exalted among the heathen, I will be exalted
in the earth.

Psalm 46:10, KJV

A heart at peace gives life to the body, but
envy rots the bones.

Proverbs 14:30, NIV

Let not your heart envy sinners, but continue
in the fear of the LORD all the day. Surely
there is a future, and your hope will not be
cut off.

Proverbs 23:17-18, ESV

A man can do nothing better than to
eat and drink and find satisfaction in his
work. This too, I see, is from the hand of
God, for without him, who can eat or find
enjoyment?

Ecclesiastes 2:24-25, NIV

Better what the eye sees than the roving
of the appetite. This too is meaningless, a
chasing after the wind.

Ecclesiastes 6:9, NIV

COURAGE

I can do all things through Christ which strengtheneth me.

Philippians 4:13, KJV

Many people cannot explain the fear that haunts them. It is understandable that the uncertain future, an incurable disease, losing your job and the death of a loved one can cause fear, but outside these things there often lurks a fear that is inexplicable. It affects the deepest stirrings of your spirit, refuses to be analysed, but is a churning presence.

There is but one sure cure for a life that is dominated by fear, and that is a living faith in Jesus Christ. Fear and faith cannot co-exist in the same life.

Faith nurtures faith and fear nurtures fear. Place your trust in God. Put God to the test, even if it is only in the little things, and you will soon find that He is actively working on the big issues in your life. When this happens, fear will subside until your whole life is free of destructive fear. You will increasingly be controlled by a positive faith and will taste success above fear.

THE COURAGE

TO COPE

"Fear not, for I am with you; be not dismayed, for I am your God. I will strengthen you, yes, I will help you, I will uphold you with My righteous right hand."

Isaiah 41:10, NKJV

But now thus says the LORD, he who created you, O Jacob, he who formed you, O Israel: "Fear not, for I have redeemed you; I have called you by name, you are mine. When you pass through the waters, I will be with you; and through the rivers, they shall not overwhelm you; when you walk through fire you shall not be burned, and the flame shall not consume you. For I am the LORD your God, the Holy One of Israel, your Savior."

Isaiah 43:1-3, ESV

Be strong and of a good courage, fear not, nor be afraid of them: for the LORD thy God, he it is that doth go with thee; he will not fail thee, nor forsake thee.

Deuteronomy 31:6, KJV

"I will pray the Father, and He will give you another Helper, that He may abide with you forever – the Spirit of truth, whom the world cannot receive, because it neither sees Him nor knows Him; but you know Him, for He dwells with you and will be in you. I will not leave you orphans; I will come to you."

John 14:16-18, NKJV

"Have I not commanded you? Be strong and courageous. Do not be frightened, and do not be dismayed, for the LORD your God is with you wherever you go."

Joshua 1:9, ESV

Do not be anxious about anything, but in everything, by prayer and petition, with thanksgiving, present your requests to God. And the peace of God, which transcends all understanding, will guard your hearts and your minds in Christ Jesus.

Philippians 4:6-7, NIV

For who is God save the LORD? or who is a rock save our God? It is God that girdeth me with strength, and maketh my way perfect.

Psalm 18:31-32, KJV

I will praise You with my whole heart; Before the gods I will sing praises to You. I will worship toward Your holy temple, And praise Your name For Your lovingkindness and Your truth; For You have magnified Your word above all Your name. In the day when I cried out, You answered me, And made me bold with strength in my soul.

Psalm 138:1-3, NKJV

The wicked flee when no one pursues, but the righteous are bold as a lion.

Proverbs 28:1, ESV

Wait on the LORD; Be of good courage, And He shall strengthen your heart; Wait, I say, on the LORD!

Psalm 27:14, NKJV

It is my eager expectation and hope that I will not be at all ashamed, but that with full courage now as always Christ will be honored in my body, whether by life or by death. For to me to live is Christ, and to die is gain.

Philippians 1:20-21, ESV

The LORD is my light and my salvation – whom shall I fear? The LORD is the stronghold of my life – of whom shall I be afraid?

Psalm 27:1, NIV

*D*EPRESSION

The LORD is a refuge for the oppressed, a stronghold in times of trouble.

Psalm 9:9, NIV

Tears are sometimes necessary so that you can see God's love and grace in your life in a new way. Just as physical tears wash the hurt from your eyes, inner hurt can help make your relationship with God more intimate. But, tears are not pleasant. Although tears are part of your life on earth, someday these tears will come to an end. The Lord wants to wipe away your tears. In Revelation 21 John writes about the new Jerusalem, the city that is going to be the home of God and His children. There the Lord will be with His children every day and there will be no more tears, because God Himself will wipe them away.

Although life on this earth is full of hurt and hardship you can hold fast to the promise that heaven, where there is no more hardship or death, mourning, sorrow or pain, is waiting for you after all your suffering.

Dealing with

Depression

And when we cried unto the LORD God of our fathers, the LORD heard our voice, and looked on our affliction, and our labour, and our oppression.

Deuteronomy 26:7, KJV

Do not let the floodwaters engulf me or the depths swallow me up or the pit close its mouth over me. Answer me, O LORD, out of the goodness of your love; in your great mercy turn to me. Do not hide your face from your servant; answer me quickly, for I am in trouble.

Psalm 69:15-17, NIV

O LORD my God, I cried out to You, and You healed me. O LORD, You brought my soul up from the grave; You have kept me alive, that I should not go down to the pit.

Psalm 30:2-3, NKJV

I will rejoice and be glad in your steadfast love, because you have seen my affliction; you have known the distress of my soul.

Psalm 31:7, ESV

My heart is sore pained within me: and the terrors of death are fallen upon me. Fearfulness and trembling are come upon me, and horror hath overwhelmed me. As for me, I will call upon God; and the LORD shall save me. Evening, and morning, and at noon, will I pray, and cry aloud: and he shall hear my voice.

Psalm 55:4-5, 16-17, KJV

Humble yourselves, therefore, under the mighty hand of God so that at the proper time he may exalt you, casting all your anxieties on him, because he cares for you.

1 Peter 5:6-7, ESV

Behold, God will not cast away the blameless, nor will He uphold the evildoers. He will yet fill your mouth with laughing, and your lips with rejoicing.

Job 8:20-21, NKJV

For the mountains shall depart, and the hills be removed; but my kindness shall not depart from thee, neither shall the covenant of my peace be removed, saith the LORD that hath mercy on thee.

Isaiah 54:10, KJV

Thou wilt not leave my soul in hell. Thou wilt shew me the path of life: in thy presence is fulness of joy; at thy right hand there are pleasures for evermore.

Psalm 16:10-11, KJV

May the God of hope fill you with all joy and peace as you trust in him, so that you may overflow with hope by the power of the Holy Spirit.

Romans 15:13, NIV

You have turned for me my mourning into dancing; you have loosed my sackcloth and clothed me with gladness, that my glory may sing your praise and not be silent. O LORD my God, I will give thanks to you forever!

Psalm 30:11-12, ESV

Do not be anxious about anything, but in everything, by prayer and petition, with thanksgiving, present your requests to God. And the peace of God, which transcends all understanding, will guard your hearts and your minds in Christ Jesus.

Philippians 4:5-7, NIV

ℰNCOURAGEMENT

*Praise be to the LORD, to God our Savior, who daily
bears our burdens.*

Psalm 68:19, NIV

When we experience adversity or misfortune, when we go through worrying times, a heavy atmosphere of doom and gloom descends upon us and the burden of anxious care becomes too much.

When you experience such feelings, it is wise to consider the wonder of God's omnipotence. There is ample testimony of His omnipotence. Evil has consistently tried to conquer good, but God's powerful hand conquered the evil one and rendered him powerless time and time again.

What seemed to be the biggest disaster, when the Son of God was nailed to a cross and died, was nullified when Christ rose triumphantly from the grave as the victor over sin, evil and death for ever.

In your dark moments consider the wonder of God's royal majesty. Be encouraged that the omnipotent Lord God reigns over everything.

Encouraging

encouragement

May our Lord Jesus Christ himself and God our Father, who loved us and by his grace gave us eternal encouragement and good hope, encourage your hearts and strengthen you in every good deed and word.

2 Thessalonians 2:16-17, NIV

The LORD is good unto them that wait for him, to the soul that seeketh him. It is good that a man should both hope and quietly wait for the salvation of the LORD.

Lamentations 3:25-26, KJV

Therefore encourage one another and build one another up, just as you are doing.

1 Thessalonians 5:11, ESV

LORD, You have heard the desire of the humble; You will prepare their heart; You will cause Your ear to hear, to do justice to the fatherless and the oppressed, that the man of the earth may oppress no more.

Psalm 10:17-18, NKJV

For I know the plans I have for you, declares the LORD, plans for wholeness and not for evil, to give you a future and a hope.

Jeremiah 29:11, ESV

He which hath begun a good work in you will perform it until the day of Jesus Christ.

Philippians 1:6, KJV

For everything that was written in the past was written to teach us, so that through endurance and the encouragement of the Scriptures we might have hope. May the God who gives endurance and encouragement give you a spirit of unity among yourselves as you follow Christ Jesus.

Romans 15:4-5, NIV

The LORD is my shepherd; I shall not want. He maketh me to lie down in green pastures: he leadeth me beside the still waters. He restoreth my soul: he leadeth me in the paths of righteousness for his name's sake. Yea, though I walk through the valley of the shadow of death, I will fear no evil: for thou art with me; thy rod and thy staff they comfort me.

Psalm 23:1-4, KJV

Let us consider how to stir up one another to love and good works, not neglecting to meet together, as is the habit of some, but encouraging one another, and all the more as you see the Day drawing near.

Hebrews 10:24-25, ESV

Cast your burden on the LORD, and he will sustain you; he will never permit the righteous to be moved.

Psalm 55:22, ESV

Because God wanted to make the unchanging nature of his purpose very clear to the heirs of what was promised, he confirmed it with an oath. God did this so that, by two unchangeable things in which it is impossible for God to lie, we who have fled to take hold of the hope offered to us may be greatly encouraged. We have this hope as an anchor for the soul, firm and secure.

Hebrews 6:17-19, NIV

"Let not your heart be troubled; you believe in God, believe also in Me. I will come again and receive you to Myself; that where I am, there you may be also."

John 14:1, 3, NKJV

$\mathcal{F}$AITH

Jesus saith unto him, Thomas, because thou hast seen me, thou hast believed: blessed are they that have not seen, and yet have believed.

John 20:29, KJV

Your faith will prove itself to be ineffective if it does not lead you to a more profound knowledge and awareness of God. An intimate relationship with Jesus Christ and sincere love for Him makes His presence a living reality for you. A positive faith in the resurrected and exalted Savior forms the basis of all Christian doctrines.

Faith becomes alive and meaningful when it is expressed through love. Without love, faith is constrained and bigoted and then the height, depth and the eternal nature of God's love cannot be fathomed or experienced.

When you possess a living faith that manifests itself in love, you have the basic qualities of a practical, inspired and effective Christianity that is acceptable to God. This then becomes a source of blessing, not only for you, but also for your fellowman.

Faith from
the Word

I pray that out of his glorious riches he may strengthen you with power through his Spirit in your inner being, so that Christ may dwell in your hearts through faith.

Ephesians 3:16-17, NIV

Trust in the LORD, and do good; dwell in the land and befriend faithfulness. Delight yourself in the LORD, and he will give you the desires of your heart. Commit your way to the LORD; trust in him, and he will act. He will bring forth your righteousness as the light, and your justice as the noonday.

Psalm 37:3-6, ESV

Blessed is the man that trusteth in the LORD, and whose hope the LORD is. For he shall be as a tree planted by the waters, and that spreadeth out her roots by the river, and shall not see when heat cometh, but her leaf shall be green; and shall not be careful in the year of drought, neither shall cease from yielding fruit.

Jeremiah 17:7-8, KJV

Now faith is the assurance of things hoped for, the conviction of things not seen.

Hebrews 11:1, ESV

Jesus answered and said to them, "Have faith in God. For assuredly, I say to you, whoever says to this mountain, 'Be removed and be cast into the sea,' and does not doubt in his heart, but believes that those things he says will be done, he will have whatever he says. Therefore I say to you whatever things you ask when you pray, believe that you receive them, and you will have them."

Mark 11:22-24, NKJV

For by grace you have been saved through faith. And this is not your own doing; it is the gift of God, not a result of works, so that no one may boast.

Ephesians 2:8-9, ESV

This righteousness from God comes through faith in Jesus Christ to all who believe.

Romans 3:22, NIV

I know whom I have believed and am per-suaded that He is able to keep what I have committed to Him until that Day.

2 Timothy 1:12, NKJV

"Truly, truly, I say to you, whoever believes has eternal life."

John 6:47, ESV

Beloved, if our heart does not condemn us, we have confidence toward God. And whatever we ask we receive from Him, because we keep His commandments and do those things that are pleasing in His sight. And this is His commandment: that we should believe on the name of His Son Jesus Christ and love one another, as He gave us commandment.

1 John 3:21-23, NKJV

Faith comes from hearing, and hearing through the word of Christ.

Romans 10:17, ESV

You are all sons of God through faith in Christ Jesus.

Galatians 3:26, NKJV

To him give all the prophets witness, that through his name whosoever believeth in him shall receive remission of sins.

Acts 10:43, KJV

AMILY

A father of the fatherless, and a judge of the widows, is God in his holy habitation. God setteth the solitary in families.

Psalm 68:5-6, KJV

Parents are to be God's representatives to their children. And God wants this authority to be acknowledged.

Today it seems as if children no longer really value the biblical structure of authority. They want to do their own thing in their own way. They want to do as their friends do. But God Himself appoints parents to lead their children and it is His will that children honor and obey their parents. If they fail to do this, it is unlikely that they will respect God or other people.

Make sure that you maintain the kind of atmosphere in your home that encourages your children to honor you and acknowledge your authority. God makes a beautiful promise to those children who acknowledge the authority of their parents: " ... *so that you may live long in the land the LORD your God is giving you*" (Ex. 20:12, NIV).

GOD'S VIEW

ON FAMILY

My son, hear the instruction of thy father, and forsake not the law of thy mother: For they shall be an ornament of grace unto thy head, and chains about thy neck.

Proverbs 1:8-9, KJV

On you was I cast from my birth, and from my mother's womb you have been my God.

Psalm 22:10, ESV

Children's children are the crown of old men; and the glory of children are their fathers.

Proverbs 17:6, KJV

My son, keep your father's command, and do not forsake the law of your mother. Bind them continually upon your heart; tie them around your neck. When you roam, they will lead you; when you sleep, they will keep you; and when you awake, they will speak with you.

Proverbs 6:20-22, NKJV

"Honor your father and your mother, so that you may live long in the land the LORD your God is giving you."

Exodus 20:12, NIV

"Whoever does the will of God, he is my brother and sister and mother."

Mark 3:35, ESV

Train up a child in the way he should go: and when he is old, he will not depart from it.

Proverbs 22:6, KJV

"If a son asks for bread from any father among you, will he give him a stone? Or if he asks for a fish, will he give him a serpent instead of a fish? Or if he asks for an egg, will he offer him a scorpion? If you then, being evil, know how to give good gifts to your children, how much more will your heavenly Father give the Holy Spirit to those who ask Him!"

Luke 11:11-13, NKJV

Her children arise and call her blessed; her husband also, and he praises her: "Many women do noble things, but you surpass them all."

Proverbs 31:28-29, NIV

The rod and reproof give wisdom, but a child left to himself brings shame to his mother.

Proverbs 29:15, ESV

The father of a righteous man has great joy; he who has a wise son delights in him. May your father and mother be glad; may she who gave you birth rejoice!

Proverbs 23:24-25, NIV

Lo, children are an heritage of the LORD: and the fruit of the womb is his reward. As arrows are in the hand of a mighty man; so are children of the youth. Happy is the man that hath his quiver full of them: they shall not be ashamed, but they shall speak with the enemies in the gate. A Song of degrees. Blessed is every one that feareth the LORD; that walketh in his ways.

Psalm 127:3-128:1, KJV

And these words which I command you today shall be in your heart. You shall teach them diligently to your children, and shall talk of them when you sit in your house, when you walk by the way, when you lie down, and when you rise up.

Deuteronomy 6:6-7, NKJV

FATIGUE

"For I have satiated the weary soul, and I have replenished every sorrowful soul."

Jeremiah 31:25, NKJV

Even though He was sometimes very tired and mostly very busy, Jesus always made time to communicate with His Father. In this way He received strength to do the things that His Father asked of Him.

The times that Jesus spent in prayer gave direction to His life. Before He selected His disciples, He prayed; before He died on the cross, He prayed. For these times of prayer, Jesus made time specially to be alone with His Father.

You too should make time to be alone with God. It is very important for you to set apart enough time in your busy daily schedule to meet with God: time for Bible study and time to pray.

Set apart a special time and place where you can communicate with your heavenly Father in solitude. In His presence you, like Jesus when He was on earth, will find enough power for all the tasks waiting for you.

Refreshment when

fatigued

So we do not lose heart. Though our outer nature is wasting away, our inner nature is being renewed day by day.

2 Corinthians 4:16, ESV

The everlasting God, the LORD, the Creator of the ends of the earth, neither faints nor is weary. His understanding is unsearchable. He gives power to the weak, and to those who have no might He increases strength. Even the youths shall faint and be weary, and the young men shall utterly fall, but those who wait on the LORD shall renew their strength; they shall mount up with wings like eagles, they shall run and not be weary, they shall walk and not faint.

Isaiah 40:28-31, NKJV

Behold, I am the LORD, the God of all flesh: is there any thing too hard for me?

Jeremiah 32:27, KJV

Trust in the LORD forever, for the LORD GOD is an everlasting rock.

Isaiah 26:4, ESV

"Come unto me, all ye that labour and are heavy laden, and I will give you rest. Take my yoke upon you, and learn of me; for I am meek and lowly in heart: and ye shall find rest unto your souls. For my yoke is easy, and my burden is light."

Matthew 11:28-30, KJV

And he said unto me, My grace is sufficient for thee: for my strength is made perfect in weakness. Most gladly therefore will I rather glory in my infirmities, that the power of Christ may rest upon me.

2 Corinthians 12:9, KJV

The LORD God is my strength; He will make my feet like deer's feet, and He will make me walk on my high hills.

Habakkuk 3:19, NKJV

The LORD will give strength unto his people; the LORD will bless his people with peace.

Psalm 29:11, KJV

My God shall supply all your need according to His riches in glory by Christ Jesus.

Philippians 4:19, NKJV

My flesh and my heart may fail, but God is the strength of my heart and my portion forever.

Psalm 73:26, ESV

Be strong in the Lord and in the power of His might.

Ephesians 6:10, NKJV

I will lift up mine eyes unto the hills, from whence cometh my help. My help cometh from the LORD, which made heaven and earth.

Psalm 121:1-2, KJV

The eternal God is your refuge, and underneath are the everlasting arms.

Deuteronomy 33:27, NIV

Fear not, for I am with you; be not dismayed, for I am your God; I will strengthen you, I will help you, I will uphold you with my righteous right hand.

Isaiah 41:10, ESV

I can do all things through Christ which strengtheneth me.

Philippians 4:13, KJV

$\mathcal{F}$INANCES

Better is little with the fear of the LORD than great treasure and trouble therewith.

Proverbs 15:16, KJV

Many people make wealth and possessions the first priority in their lives. Wealth in itself is no sin, just as poverty per se is no virtue. But the rich man must regard his wealth as a transitory trust that should not be used for his own selfish ends. The issue is how you can use it to best serve your fellow-man. What matters is not the money that you possess, but the motivation for it and the way in which it is spent. True wealth enriches those with whom you come into contact, because you are not giving only of your money, but of yourself as well.

To share in the blessings of God, means that you must also live in fellowship with Him so that His standards become your standards. It is only when everything that you possess is dedicated to your Lord and Master, and when you use it to His honor and with His holy purpose in mind, that you possess true wealth.

The Word's view

on finances

Better is the little that the righteous has than the abundance of many wicked.

Psalm 37:16, ESV

"Give, and it shall be given unto you; good measure, pressed down, and shaken together, and running over, shall men give into your bosom. For with the same measure that ye mete withal it shall be measured to you again."

Luke 6:38, KJV

Remember the LORD your God, for it is he who gives you the ability to produce wealth, and so confirms his covenant.

Deuteronomy 8:18, NIV

My God will meet all your needs according to his glorious riches in Christ Jesus.

Philippians 4:19, NIV

Honor the LORD with your wealth and with the firstfruits of all your produce; then your barns will be filled with plenty, and your vats will be bursting with wine.

Proverbs 3:9-10, ESV

Labour not to be rich: cease from thine own wisdom. Wilt thou set thine eyes upon that which is not? for riches certainly make themselves wings; they fly away as an eagle toward heaven.

Proverbs 23:4-5, KJV

Keep your lives free from the love of money and be content with what you have, because God has said, "Never will I leave you; never will I forsake you."

Hebrews 13:5, NIV

As for the rich in this present age, charge them not to be haughty, nor to set their hopes on the uncertainty of riches, but on God, who richly provides us with everything to enjoy. They are to do good, to be rich in good works, to be generous and ready to share, thus storing up treasure for themselves as a good foundation for the future, so that they may take hold of that which is truly life.

1 Timothy 6:17-19, ESV

He who loves silver will not be satisfied with silver; nor he who loves abundance, with increase. This also is vanity.

Ecclesiastes 5:10, NKJV

Bring the full tithes into the storehouse, that there may be food in my house. And thereby put me to the test, says the LORD of hosts, if I will not open the windows of heaven for you and pour down for you a blessing until there is no more need.

Malachi 3:10, ESV

"Do not worry, saying, 'What shall we eat?' or 'What shall we drink?' or 'What shall we wear?' For after all these things the Gentiles seek. For your heavenly Father knows that you need all these things."

Matthew 6:31-32, NKJV

Each man should give what he has decided in his heart to give, not reluctantly or under compulsion, for God loves a cheerful giver. And God is able to make all grace abound to you, so that in all things at all times, having all that you need, you will abound in every good work.

2 Corinthians 9:7-8, NIV

Everyone also to whom God has given wealth and possessions and power to enjoy them, and to accept his lot and rejoice in his toil – this is the gift of God.

Ecclesiastes 5:19, ESV

$\mathcal{F}$ORGIVENESS

Thou hast forgiven the iniquity of thy people, thou hast covered all their sin.

Psalm 85:2, KJV

It is one of life's great arts to know what to forget and what to remember. People become collectors of grievances and this poisons their souls and drives the love from their hearts.

Many people nurture their anger to keep it glowing; they brood on the mistakes made against them. Then the grievance begets a whole string of little ones. Later, it becomes impossible for them to forget. Christ taught the great lesson of forgetting *and* forgiving. If you keep record of the wrongs committed against you, you are inclined to miss the noble, good and beautiful things in life.

This takes us back to the point of departure for all of this: the ability to forgive. If you cannot forgive, you keep record of the wrongs; if you keep record of the wrongs, you gradually lose Christian love from your heart.

God's promises

of forgiveness

"When you stand praying, if you hold anything against anyone, forgive him, so that your Father in heaven may forgive you your sins."

Mark 11:25, NIV

"But I say unto you, Love your enemies, bless them that curse you, do good to them that hate you, and pray for them which despitefully use you, and persecute you; That ye may be the children of your Father which is in heaven: for he maketh his sun to rise on the evil and on the good, and sendeth rain on the just and on the unjust."

Matthew 5:44-45, KJV

"For if you forgive men their trespasses, your heavenly Father will also forgive you. But if you do not forgive men their trespasses, neither will your Father forgive your trespasses."

Matthew 6:14-15, NKJV

Do not say, "I will repay evil"; wait for the LORD, and he will deliver you.

Proverbs 20:22, ESV

Create in me a clean heart, O God; and renew a right spirit within me. Cast me not away from thy presence; and take not thy holy spirit from me. Restore unto me the joy of thy salvation; and uphold me with thy free spirit.

Psalm 51:10-12, KJV

I acknowledged my sin to you, and I did not cover my iniquity; I said, "I will confess my transgressions to the LORD," and you forgave the iniquity of my sin.

Psalm 32:5, ESV

I write to you, dear children, because your sins have been forgiven on account of his name.

1 John 2:12, NIV

Who is a God like You, pardoning iniquity and passing over the transgression of the remnant of His heritage? He does not retain His anger forever, because He delights in mercy.

Micah 7:18, NKJV

"Judge not, and ye shall not be judged: condemn not, and ye shall not be condemned: forgive, and ye shall be forgiven."

Luke 6:37, KJV

Bless those who persecute you; bless and do not curse.

Romans 12:14, NIV

If we confess our sins, he is faithful and just to forgive us our sins and to cleanse us from all unrighteousness.

1 John 1:9, ESV

"Lord, how often shall my brother sin against me, and I forgive him? Up to seven times?" Jesus said to him, "I do not say to you, up to seven times, but up to seventy times seven."

Matthew 18:21-22, NKJV

And you, being dead in your trespasses and the uncircumcision of your flesh, He has made alive together with Him, having forgiven you all trespasses, having wiped out the handwriting of requirements that was against us, which was contrary to us. And He has taken it out of the way, having nailed it to the cross.

Colossians 2:13-14, NKJV

In him we have redemption through his blood, the forgiveness of our trespasses, according to the riches of his grace.

Ephesians 1:7, ESV

FRIENDS

Bear one another's burdens, and so fulfill the law of Christ.

Galatians 6:2, NKJV

Let us thank God for those people who take pleasure in helping others. No task is too small for them, and they rejoice in doing good. They do not seek any reward, except for making life richer and easier for their fellowmen. To forget about yourself in the service of others, is the path to a full and satisfying life.

Find somebody who is in need. A lonely person might welcome friendship; someone who is confused will appreciate an understanding listener; a single mother might welcome a responsible child-minder so that she can go out for an evening. There are so many different ways in which to help. While you are helping others, you will receive a rich blessing as your reward. Every good deed that is performed in the Name of Christ bestows a blessing on both the donor and the receiver. Most of all, it brings glory to His Name.

Friends for
the friendly

They kissed one another; and they wept together, but David more so. Then Jonathan said to David, "Go in peace, since we have both sworn in the name of the LORD, saying, 'May the LORD be between you and me, and between your descendants and my descendants, forever.'"

1 Samuel 20:41-42, NKJV

A man that hath friends must shew himself friendly: and there is a friend that sticketh closer than a brother.

Proverbs 18:24, KJV

"Greater love has no one than this, that someone lays down his life for his friends. You are my friends if you do what I command you."

John 15:13-14, ESV

Two are better than one, because they have a good return for their work: If one falls down, his friend can help him up. But pity the man who falls and has no one to help him up!

Ecclesiastes 4:9-10, NIV

Do not forsake your own friend or your father's friend, nor go to your brother's house in the day of your calamity; better is a neighbor nearby than a brother far away.

Proverbs 27:10, NKJV

"He who withholds kindness from a friend forsakes the fear of the Almighty."

Job 6:14, ESV

Now when Job's three friends heard of all this evil that had come upon him, they came each from his own place. They made an appointment together to come to show him sympathy and comfort him.

Job 2:11, ESV

"Go home to your friends and tell them how much the Lord has done for you, and how he has had mercy on you."

Mark 5:19, ESV

"Do to others as you would have them do to you."

Luke 6:31, NIV

Perfume and incense bring joy to the heart, and the pleasantness of one's friend springs from his earnest counsel.

Proverbs 27:9, NIV

A righteous man is cautious in friendship, but the way of the wicked leads them astray.

Proverbs 12:26, NIV

After Job had prayed for his friends, the LORD made him prosperous again and gave him twice as much as he had before.

Job 42:10, NIV

And let us consider one another in order to stir up love and good works, not forsaking the assembling of ourselves together, as is the manner of some, but exhorting one another, and so much the more as you see the Day approaching.

Hebrews 10:24-25, NKJV

He who covers over an offense promotes love, but whoever repeats the matter separates close friends.

Proverbs 17:9, NIV

Above all, love each other deeply, because love covers over a multitude of sins.

1 Peter 4:8, NIV

$\mathcal{G}$OD

O LORD, you are our Father. We are the clay, you are the potter; we are all the work of your hand.
Isaiah 64:8, NIV

The Lord is good. That is the all-important fact. It is a truth to sing about, and sing about in days of darkness, for though the light of God's countenance appears hidden for a moment, this quality remains forever. God is good.

Because God is good, certain things follow. His mercy endures forever, He is our refuge and strength, a very present help in trouble. God's mercy is His goodness extended to us in our sin or need, and because God endures, His goodness and mercy likewise endure.

If we hold fast to this, then we shall find in Him a place of retreat and defense, whatever experiences we may pass through. The Lord not only loves us, but He knows us, knows our ways most intimately.

The result of realizing God's goodness and His knowledge is surely to make us long to walk before Him in holiness all our days.

The Word's view
on God

For he is our God, and we are the people of
his pasture, and the sheep of his hand.

Psalm 95:7, ESV

I said to the LORD, "You are my Lord; apart
from you I have no good thing."

Psalm 16:2, NIV

"Great and marvelous are your deeds, Lord
God Almighty. Just and true are your ways,
King of the ages."

Revelation 15:3, NIV

"I will be a Father to you, and you shall
be My sons and daughters, says the Lord
Almighty."

2 Corinthians 6:18, NKJV

For the LORD God is a sun and shield; the
LORD bestows favor and honor. No good
thing does he withhold from those who
walk uprightly.

Psalm 84:11, ESV

For I am the LORD thy God, the Holy One of Israel, thy Saviour.

Isaiah 43:3, KJV

"For God so loved the world, that he gave his only Son, that whoever believes in him should not perish but have eternal life."

John 3:16, ESV

But if anybody does sin, we have one who speaks to the Father in our defense – Jesus Christ, the Righteous One. He is the atoning sacrifice for our sins, and not only for ours but also for the sins of the whole world.

1 John 2:1-2, NIV

Blessed be the God and Father of our Lord Jesus Christ, the Father of mercies and God of all comfort.

2 Corinthians 1:3, NKJV

"The Rock, his work is perfect, for all his ways are justice. A God of faithfulness and without iniquity, just and upright is he."

Deuteronomy 32:4, ESV

"I know that you can do all things, and that no purpose of yours can be thwarted."

Job 42:2, ESV

But to us there is but one God, the Father, of whom are all things, and we in him; and one Lord Jesus Christ, by whom are all things, and we by him.

1 Corinthians 8:6, KJV

"The LORD, the LORD God, merciful and gracious, longsuffering, and abounding in goodness and truth, keeping mercy for thousands, forgiving iniquity and transgression and sin."

Exodus 34:6-7, NKJV

Oh, the depth of the riches of the wisdom and knowledge of God! How unsearchable his judgments, and his paths beyond tracing out!

Romans 11:33, NIV

Before the mountains were brought forth, or ever thou hadst formed the earth and the world, even from everlasting to everlasting, thou art God.

Psalm 90:2, KJV

Now to the King eternal, immortal, invisible, to God who alone is wise, be honor and glory forever and ever. Amen.

1 Timothy 1:17, NKJV

GOSSIP

Deliver me, O LORD, from lying lips, from a deceitful tongue.

Psalm 120:2, ESV

How words are spoken is of utmost importance. A wrong word and bad timing can have a devastating effect on someone's life.

There are times when people yearn for a word of encouragement or compassion, and an expression of love or interest can brighten their day. A word of praise is never wasted; even constructive criticism or a concerned reprimand can be beneficial to the receiver.

The most important thing is that, through the power of the Holy Spirit, you should choose your words wisely and determine their timing with responsibility and care. Be sensitive to the person you talk to. Avoid needless flattery as well as heartlessness. Always be sincere in what you say and speak with the love of Jesus Christ in your heart. In this way you will enrich not only the life of the person you are talking to, but your own life too.

THE WORD'S VIEW

ON GOSSIP

He that goeth about as a talebearer revealeth secrets: therefore meddle not with him that flattereth with his lips.

Proverbs 20:19, KJV

Now you must rid yourselves of all such things as these: anger, rage, malice, slander, and filthy language from your lips.

Colossians 3:8, NIV

The words of a gossip are like choice morsels; they go down to a man's inmost parts.

Proverbs 18:8, NIV

LORD, who may dwell in your sanctuary? Who may live on your holy hill? He whose walk is blameless and who does what is righteous, who speaks the truth from his heart and has no slander on his tongue, who does his neighbor no wrong and casts no slur on his fellowman.

Psalm 15:1-3, NIV

Thou shalt not bear false witness against thy neighbour.

Exodus 20:16, KJV

"Whoever desires to love life and see good days, let him keep his tongue from evil and his lips from speaking deceit."

1 Peter 3:10, ESV

Put away from thee a froward mouth, and perverse lips put far from thee.

Proverbs 4:24, KJV

"Do not go about spreading slander among your people. Do not do anything that endangers your neighbor's life. I am the LORD."

Leviticus 19:16, NKJV

Without wood a fire goes out; without gossip a quarrel dies down. As charcoal to embers and as wood to fire, so is a quarrelsome man for kindling strife. The words of a gossip are like choice morsels; they go down to a man's inmost parts.

Proverbs 26:20-22, NIV

Death and life are in the power of the tongue, and those who love it will eat its fruits.

Proverbs 18:21, ESV

Keep thy tongue from evil, and thy lips from speaking guile.

Psalm 34:13, KJV

Therefore, having put away falsehood, let each one of you speak the truth with his neighbor, for we are members one of another.

Ephesians 4:25, ESV

Like a club or a sword or a sharp arrow is the man who gives false testimony against his neighbor.

Proverbs 25:18, NIV

"Do not spread false reports. Do not help a wicked man by being a malicious witness."

Exodus 23:1, NIV

The lip of truth shall be established for ever: but a lying tongue is but for a moment.

Proverbs 12:19, KJV

And above all things have fervent love for one another, for "love will cover a multitude of sins."

1 Peter 4:8, NKJV

GRACE

God opposes the proud, but gives grace to the humble.

James 4:6, ESV

Grace is the unmerited favor of God; it is such favor adapting itself to our personal needs. It describes the disposition of a loving but holy God toward His sinful and undeserving creatures. Let us think for a moment of this grace, for if we begin to understand it, we shall appreciate it, and if we appreciate it we shall all the more adore and love the God of all grace.

God has taken the initiative and dealt with our sins. He now offers pardon and peace and power to the sons of men. God's grace is abundant, there is no hesitation or limitation in the pardon; there is no shadow about the acceptance; and there is no restriction in the resources which are now ours in Christ Jesus.

And all of God's gifts to me I claim
I dare believe in Jesus' name.

GOD'S GLORIOUS GRACE

God is able to make all grace abound toward you, that you, always having all sufficiency in all things, may have an abundance for every good work.

2 Corinthians 9:8, NKJV

But by the grace of God I am what I am: and his grace which was bestowed upon me was not in vain; but I laboured more abundantly than they all: yet not I, but the grace of God which was with me.

1 Corinthians 15:10, KJV

But after that the kindness and love of God our Saviour toward man appeared, Not by works of righteousness which we have done, but according to his mercy he saved us, by the washing of regeneration, and renewing of the Holy Ghost; Which he shed on us abundantly through Jesus Christ our Saviour; That being justified by his grace, we should be made heirs according to the hope of eternal life.

Titus 3:4-7, KJV

But grace was given to each one of us according to the measure of Christ's gift.

Ephesians 4:7, ESV

But God, who is rich in mercy, because of His great love with which He loved us, even when we were dead in trespasses, made us alive together with Christ (by grace you have been saved), and raised us up together, and made us sit together in the heavenly places in Christ Jesus, that in the ages to come He might show the exceeding riches of His grace in His kindness toward us in Christ Jesus. For by grace you have been saved through faith, and that not of yourselves; it is the gift of God, not of works, lest anyone should boast.

Ephesians 2:4-9, NKJV

Let us then with confidence draw near to the throne of grace, that we may receive mercy and find grace to help in time of need.

Hebrews 4:16, ESV

All have sinned and fall short of the glory of God, and are justified freely by his grace through the redemption that came by Christ Jesus.

Romans 3:23-24, NIV

We believe that through the grace of the Lord Jesus Christ we shall be saved.

Acts 15:11, NKJV

But he said to me, "My grace is sufficient for you, for my power is made perfect in weakness." Therefore I will boast all the more gladly of my weaknesses, so that the power of Christ may rest upon me.

2 Corinthians 12:9, ESV

In Him we have redemption through His blood, the forgiveness of sins, according to the riches of His grace which He made to abound toward us in all wisdom and prudence.

Ephesians 1:7-8, NKJV

Each one should use whatever gift he has received to serve others, faithfully administering God's grace in its various forms.

1 Peter 4:10, NIV

And from his fullness we have all received, grace upon grace. For the law was given through Moses; grace and truth came through Jesus Christ.

John 1:16-17, ESV

GRATITUDE

O give thanks unto the LORD; for he is good; for his mercy endureth for ever.

1 Chronicles 16:34, KJV

Disciples should be grateful people, people who are attuned to all the wonderful things that God gives and does for them in His grace. We should thank God for each of His blessings. The word "everything" indicates that we should also give thanks for those things that are disagreeable to us, but nevertheless that the Lord wants to use positively in our lives. He can make all things, even suffering and hardship, work for our good.

When last did you thank the Lord not only for all the great and wonderful gifts that He gives you, but also for all the small, insignificant things that you so often take for granted? Always remember that you don't deserve anything that you receive from Him. Everything you have, comes only from the grace of God. Be aware of God's blessings in your life and make a point of thanking Him for them every day.

Developing

GRATITUDE

First of all, then, I urge that supplications, prayers, intercessions, and thanksgivings be made for all people, for kings and all who are in high positions, that we may lead a peaceful and quiet life, godly and dignified in every way.

1 Timothy 2:1-2, ESV

So then, just as you received Christ Jesus as Lord, continue to live in him, rooted and built up in him, strengthened in the faith as you were taught, and overflowing with thankfulness.

Colossians 2:6-7, NIV

Let us come before his presence with thanksgiving, and make a joyful noise unto him with Psalms. For the LORD is a great God, and a great King above all gods.

Psalm 95:2-3, KJV

Whatever you do, whether in word or deed, do it all in the name of the Lord Jesus, giving thanks to God the Father through him.

Colossians 3:17, NIV

Rejoice always, pray without ceasing, give thanks in all circumstances; for this is the will of God in Christ Jesus for you.

1 Thessalonians 5:16-18, ESV

Oh, give thanks to the LORD, for He is good! For His mercy endures forever.

Psalm 107:1, NKJV

Since we are receiving a kingdom that cannot be shaken, let us be thankful, and so worship God acceptably with reverence and awe.

Hebrews 12:28, NIV

Be careful for nothing; but in every thing by prayer and supplication with thanksgiving let your requests be made known unto God.

Philippians 4:6, KJV

Give thanks to the LORD, call on his name; make known among the nations what he has done.

1 Chronicles 16:8, NIV

My heart greatly rejoiceth; and with my song will I praise him.

Psalm 28:7, KJV

Let them thank the LORD for his steadfast love, for his wondrous works to the children of men! And let them offer sacrifices of thanksgiving, and tell of his deeds in songs of joy!

Psalm 107:21-22, ESV

Enter into His gates with thanksgiving, And into His courts with praise. Be thankful to Him, and bless His name. For the LORD is good; His mercy is everlasting.

Psalm 100:4-5, NKJV

We give thanks to you, O God; we give thanks, for your name is near. We recount your wondrous deeds.

Psalm 75:1, ESV

Let the word of Christ dwell in you richly as you teach and admonish one another with all wisdom, and as you sing psalms, hymns and spiritual songs with gratitude in your hearts to God.

Colossians 3:16, NIV

Always giving thanks to God the Father for everything, in the name of our Lord Jesus Christ.

Ephesians 5:20, NIV

$\mathcal{G}$UIDANCE

I am continually with You; You hold me by my right hand. You will guide me with Your counsel, and afterward receive me to glory.

Psalm 73:23-24, NKJV

Each of us chooses for ourselves what we want to be and where we want to go. This choice involves much more than wishful thinking. And this is where the acceptance of Christ as Lord of your life puts divine powers into action.

Choosing your objectives with Christ's help causes you to put your feet on a road that you can follow with a clear conscience. It will bring joy, confidence and enthusiasm into your life. A by-product of such a way of living is that the relationship between you and the triune God becomes more intimate. Striving to reach the goal then becomes just as joyful as its attainment. If you walk your path of life in the light of God, the whole journey becomes a joyous experience.

GUIDANCE FROM THE WORD

Trust in the LORD with all thine heart; and lean not unto thine own understanding. In all thy ways acknowledge him, and he shall direct thy paths.

Proverbs 3:5-6, KJV

Teach me to do your will, for you are my God; may your good Spirit lead me on level ground.

Psalm 143:10, NIV

Let the word of Christ dwell in you richly, teaching and admonishing one another in all wisdom, singing Psalms and hymns and spiritual songs, with thankfulness in your hearts to God.

Colossians 3:16, ESV

If any of you lacks wisdom, he should ask God, who gives generously to all without finding fault, and it will be given to him. But when he asks, he must believe and not doubt.

James 1:5-6, NIV

Teach me good judgment and knowledge: for I have believed thy commandments.

Psalm 119:66, KJV

"When He, the Spirit of truth, has come, He will guide you into all truth; for He will not speak on His own authority, but whatever He hears He will speak; and He will tell you things to come."

John 16:13, NKJV

And the LORD shall guide thee continually, and satisfy thy soul in drought, and make fat thy bones: and thou shalt be like a watered garden, and like a spring of water, whose waters fail not.

Isaiah 58:11, KJV

Your word is a lamp to my feet and a light to my path.

Psalm 119:105, ESV

And thine ears shall hear a word behind thee, saying, This is the way, walk ye in it, when ye turn to the right hand, and when ye turn to the left.

Isaiah 30:21, KJV

He leads the humble in what is right, and teaches the humble his way. All the paths of the LORD are steadfast love and faithfulness, for those who keep his covenant and his testimonies.

Psalm 25:9-10, ESV

By a pillar of cloud you led them in the day, and by a pillar of fire in the night to light for them the way in which they should go.

Nehemiah 9:12, ESV

For thou art my rock and my fortress; therefore for thy name's sake lead me, and guide me.

Psalm 31:3, KJV

Send forth your light and your truth, let them guide me; let them bring me to your holy mountain, to the place where you dwell.

Psalm 43:3, NIV

And I will give you shepherds according to My heart, who will feed you with knowledge and understanding.

Jeremiah 3:15, NKJV

GUILT

Your guilt is taken away and your sin atoned for.
Isaiah 6:7, NIV

When people are oppressed by their feelings of guilt, they often become so depressed that they withdraw into themselves. Eventually they break down under the burden they carry. To prevent yourself from succumbing to the destructive effect of guilt, you must acknowledge and accept that God, because He loves you so very much, has taken your sins upon Himself in Christ, and died on the cross in your stead. You received divine forgiveness and can be assured of redemption through the blood of the Lamb.

God's love for you is so boundless that He is always willing to listen to your confession of guilt and to take you back through His forgiving love.

Why torture yourself with feelings of guilt while His endless love is available for you? There is only one way to answer His love, and that is by loving Him in return. When you are set free from your guilt you will be able to live a life of love to His honor.

GOD FORGIVES

OUR GUILT

For the LORD your God is gracious and merciful, and will not turn away his face from you, if ye return unto him.

2 Chronicles 30:9, KJV

Then I acknowledged my sin to you and did not cover up my iniquity. I said, "I will confess my transgressions to the LORD" – and you forgave the guilt of my sin.

Psalm 32:5, NIV

As far as the east is from the west, so far does he remove our transgressions from us.

Psalm 103:12, ESV

For if our heart condemns us, God is greater than our heart, and knows all things.

1 John 3:20, NKJV

And I will cleanse them from all their iniquity, whereby they have sinned against me; and I will pardon all their iniquities, whereby they have sinned, and whereby they have transgressed against me.

Jeremiah 33:8, KJV

"I will forgive their wickedness and will remember their sins no more."

Hebrews 8:12, NIV

If we confess our sins, He is faithful and just to forgive us our sins and to cleanse us from all unrighteousness.

1 John 1:9, NKJV

For our sake he made him to be sin who knew no sin, so that in him we might become the righteousness of God.

2 Corinthians 5:21, ESV

There is therefore now no condemnation to those who are in Christ Jesus, who do not walk according to the flesh, but according to the Spirit. For the law of the Spirit of life in Christ Jesus has made me free from the law of sin and death.

Romans 8:1-2, NKJV

"Blessed are those whose lawless deeds are forgiven, and whose sins are covered; blessed is the man against whom the Lord will not count his sin."

Romans 4:7-8, ESV

GUILT

Have mercy on me, O God, according to your steadfast love; according to your abundant mercy blot out my transgressions. Wash me thoroughly from my iniquity, and cleanse me from my sin! For I know my transgressions, and my sin is ever before me. Against you, you only, have I sinned and done what is evil in your sight, so that you may be justified in your words and blameless in your judgment.

Psalm 51:1-4, ESV

And she will bring forth a Son, and you shall call His name Jesus, for He will save His people from their sins.

Matthew 1:21, NKJV

For the wages of sin is death; but the gift of God is eternal life through Jesus Christ our Lord.

Romans 6:23, KJV

God exalted him to his own right hand as Prince and Savior that he might give repentance and forgiveness of sins to Israel.

Acts 5:31, NIV

$\mathcal{H}$EAVEN

Nevertheless we, according to his promise, look for new heavens and a new earth, wherein dwelleth righteousness.

2 *Peter* 3:13, KJV

Eye has not seen, nor ear heard, neither has it entered into the heart of man to conceive the things which God has laid up for us who love Him but God has revealed them to us. In heaven all God's creatures, the angelic hosts and the spirits of just men made perfect, always do all that God the Father wills. This makes heaven what it is.

When the Lord Jesus came down to earth He came to live a heavenly life here among men, and that meant doing the will of God from the heart, and we who follow Him are called to the same high objective.

This wonderfully simplifies life for it reduces the principles of conduct and behavior to a single principle, and though it may not always be easy either to discover or do God's will, yet if our eye be single we shall know it, and if our intention be pure we shall be helped in fulfilling it.

THE PROMISES

OF HEAVEN

Praise be to the God and Father of our Lord Jesus Christ! In his great mercy he has given us new birth into a living hope through the resurrection of Jesus Christ from the dead, and into an inheritance that can never perish, spoil or fade – kept in heaven for you.

1 Peter 1:3-4, NIV

"Lay up for yourselves treasures in heaven, where neither moth nor rust destroys and where thieves do not break in and steal. For where your treasure is, there your heart will be also."

Matthew 6:20-21, ESV

"Blessed are you when people insult you, persecute you and falsely say all kinds of evil against you because of me. Rejoice and be glad, because great is your reward in heaven."

Matthew 5:11-12, NIV

"Our Father which art in heaven, Hallowed be thy name. Thy kingdom come. Thy will be done in earth, as it is in heaven."

Matthew 6:9-10, KJV

For the Lord himself will descend from heaven with a cry of command, with the voice of an archangel, and with the sound of the trumpet of God. And the dead in Christ will rise first. Then we who are alive, who are left, will be caught up together with them in the clouds to meet the Lord in the air, and so we will always be with the Lord.

1 Thessalonians 4:16-17, ESV

Then I saw a new heaven and a new earth, for the first heaven and the first earth had passed away, and there was no longer any sea. I saw the Holy City, the new Jerusalem, coming down out of heaven from God, prepared as a bride beautifully dressed for her husband. And I heard a loud voice from the throne saying, "Now the dwelling of God is with men, and he will live with them. They will be his people, and God himself will be with them and be their God. He will wipe every tear from their eyes. There will be no more death or mourning or crying or pain, for the old order of things has passed away." He who was seated on the throne said, "I am making everything new!"

Revelation 21:1-5, NIV

For our citizenship is in heaven, from
which we also eagerly wait for the Savior,
the Lord Jesus Christ, who will transform
our lowly body that it may be conformed
to His glorious body.

Philippians 3:20-21, NKJV

Therefore know this day, and consider it in
your heart, that the Lord Himself is God
in heaven above and on the earth beneath;
there is no other.

Deuteronomy 4:39, NKJV

"In my Father's house are many mansions:
if it were not so, I would have told you. I go
to prepare a place for you. And if I go and
prepare a place for you, I will come again,
and receive you unto myself; that where I
am, there ye may be also."

John 14:2-3, KJV

For we know that if our earthly house of
this tabernacle were dissolved, we have a
building of God, an house not made with
hands, eternal in the heavens.

2 Corinthians 5:1, KJV

HOPE

The LORD taketh pleasure in them that fear him, in those that hope in his mercy.

Psalm 147:11, KJV

The person who scans the horizon, who looks ahead and believes that "hope springs eternal in the human breast" maintains a youthful spirit and leads an adventurous life. If you have already traveled far along life's road you might think there is no ground for hope. But you are alive today and this is God's precious gift to you. Make the most of every hour of every day.

Hold on to the assurance that God has saved His best for you - even if you think you are at the end of your road. As a child of God you have the hope of eternal life. Even if this life has been a struggle, even though memories of a beautiful yesterday seem to pull you back into the past, grasp this golden day that God has given to you and live it to the full and the glory of God. Keep the fire of hope burning in your heart and remember that the future holds many opportunities with God.

Hope from the Word

Through him we have also obtained access by faith into this grace in which we stand, and we rejoice in hope of the glory of God. More than that, we rejoice in our sufferings, knowing that suffering produces endurance, and endurance produces character, and character produces hope, and hope does not put us to shame, because God's love has been poured into our hearts through the Holy Spirit who has been given to us.

Romans 5:2-5, ESV

Through him you believe in God, who raised him from the dead and glorified him, and so your faith and hope are in God.

1 Peter 1:21, NIV

Blessed be the God and Father of our Lord Jesus Christ, which according to his abundant mercy hath begotten us again unto a lively hope by the resurrection of Jesus Christ from the dead.

1 Peter 1:3, KJV

Know that wisdom is such to your soul; if you find it, there will be a future, and your hope will not be cut off.

Proverbs 24:14, ESV

Wherefore gird up the loins of your mind, be sober, and hope to the end for the grace that is to be brought unto you at the Revelation of Jesus Christ.

1 Peter 1:13, KJV

We have put our hope in the living God, who is the Savior of all men, and especially of those who believe.

1 Timothy 4:10, NIV

You are my hiding place and my shield; I hope in your word.

Psalm 119:114, ESV

The LORD is good to those who wait for Him, to the soul who seeks Him. It is good that one should hope and wait quietly for the salvation of the LORD.

Lamentations 3:25-26, NKJV

For God alone, O my soul, wait in silence, for my hope is from him.

Psalm 62:5, ESV

May the God of hope fill you with all joy and peace in believing, so that by the power of the Holy Spirit you may abound in hope.

Romans 15:13, ESV

This I recall to my mind, therefore have I hope. It is of the LORD's mercies that we are not consumed, because his compassions fail not.

Lamentations 3:21-22, KJV

I have hope in God, which they themselves also accept, that there will be a resurrection of the dead, both of the just and the unjust.

Acts 24:15, NKJV

For thou art my hope, O LORD GOD: thou art my trust from my youth.

Psalm 71:5, KJV

For we were saved in this hope, but hope that is seen is not hope; for why does one still hope for what he sees? But if we hope for what we do not see, we eagerly wait for it with perseverance.

Romans 8:24-25, NKJV

$\mathcal{H}$OSPITALITY

Share with God's people who are in need. Practice hospitality.

> Romans 12:13, NIV

Hospitality is a command from God. *"Offer hospitality to one another without grumbling,"* Peter writes (1 Pet. 4:9).

Read in Genesis 18 with what hospitable abandon Abraham received his three visitors. But when we hear that somebody wants to visit us, we often think first about the time, effort, and expense it will require from us. We would much rather give money than open our homes to others.

True hospitality involves much more than this. It means that you will also be prepared to open your heart to visitors to make them feel truly welcome. We should at least try to live more hospitably toward our acquaintances; to care more for each other. We need to be more genuinely compassionate toward each other; to receive our acquaintances and friends in our homes with generous hospitality.

Showing

Hospitality

"Then said he also to him that bade him, When thou makest a dinner or a supper, call not thy friends, nor thy brethren, neither thy kinsmen, nor thy rich neighbours; lest they also bid thee again, and a recompence be made thee. But when thou makest a feast, call the poor, the maimed, the lame, the blind: And thou shalt be blessed; for they cannot recompense thee: for thou shalt be recompensed at the resurrection of the just."

Luke 14:12-14, KJV

Do not forget to entertain strangers, for by so doing some have unwittingly entertained angels.

Hebrews 13:2, NKJV

If anyone has material possessions and sees his brother in need but has no pity on him, how can the love of God be in him? Dear children, let us not love with words or tongue but with actions and in truth.

1 John 3:17-18, NIV

The LORD appeared to him by the terebinth trees of Mamre, as he was sitting in the tent door in the heat of the day. So he lifted his eyes and looked, and behold, three men were standing by him; and when he saw them, he ran from the tent door to meet them, and bowed himself to the ground, and said, "My Lord, if I have now found favor in Your sight, do not pass on by Your servant. Please let a little water be brought, and wash your feet, and rest yourselves under the tree. And I will bring a morsel of bread, that you may refresh your hearts." So Abraham hurried into the tent to Sarah and said, "Quickly, make ready three measures of fine meal; knead it and make cakes." And Abraham ran to the herd, took a tender and good calf, gave it to a young man, and he hastened to prepare it. So he took butter and milk and the calf which he had prepared, and set it before them; and he stood by them under the tree as they ate.

Genesis 18:1-8, NKJV

"And the King shall answer and say unto them, Verily I say unto you, Inasmuch as ye have done it unto one of the least of these my brethren, ye have done it unto me."

Matthew 25:40, KJV

Above all, keep loving one another earnestly, since love covers a multitude of sins. Show hospitality to one another without grumbling. As each has received a gift, use it to serve one another, as good stewards of God's varied grace.

1 Peter 4:8-10, ESV

Our desire is not that others might be relieved while you are hard pressed, but that there might be equality. At the present time your plenty will supply what they need, so that in turn their plenty will supply what you need.

2 Corinthians 8:13-14, NIV

If a brother or sister is naked and destitute of daily food, and one of you says to them, "Depart in peace, be warmed and filled," but you do not give them the things which are needed for the body, what does it profit?

James 2:15-16, NKJV

"For whosoever shall give you a cup of water to drink in my name, because ye belong to Christ, verily I say unto you, he shall not lose his reward."

Mark 9:41, KJV

$\mathcal{H}$UMILITY AND $\mathcal{P}$RIDE

By humility and the fear of the LORD are riches, and honour, and life.

Proverbs 22:4, KJV

What a solemn thought, that our love to God will be measured by our everyday fellowship with other people and the love it displays. It is even so with our humility. It is easy to think we humble ourselves before God. Yet, humility toward others will be the only sufficient proof that our humility before God is real. It will be the only proof that humility has become our very nature, that we actually, like Christ, have made ourselves of no reputation. When in the presence of God lowliness of heart has become, not a posture we assume for a time when we think of Him, or pray to Him, but the very spirit of our life, it will manifest itself in all our bearing toward our brethren.

The lesson is one of deep importance. The only humility that is really ours is not that which we try to show before God in prayer, but that which we carry with us, and carry out, in our ordinary conduct.

THE WORD'S VIEW ON

HUMILITY AND PRIDE

For thus says the High and Lofty One who inhabits eternity, whose name is Holy: "I dwell in the high and holy place, with him who has a contrite and humble spirit, to revive the spirit of the humble, and to revive the heart of the contrite ones."

Isaiah 57:15, NKJV

LORD, thou hast heard the desire of the humble: thou wilt prepare their heart, thou wilt cause thine ear to hear.

Psalm 10:17, KJV

Everything in the world – the cravings of sinful man, the lust of his eyes and the boasting of what he has and does – comes not from the Father but from the world. The world and its desires pass away, but the man who does the will of God lives forever.

1 John 2:16-17, NIV

Humble yourselves, therefore, under the mighty hand of God so that at the proper time he may exalt you.

1 Peter 5:6, ESV

The lofty looks of man shall be humbled, and the haughtiness of men shall be bowed down, and the LORD alone shall be exalted in that day.

Isaiah 2:11, KJV

One's pride will bring him low, but he who is lowly in spirit will obtain honor.

Proverbs 29:23, ESV

He guides the humble in what is right and teaches them his way.

Psalm 25:9, NIV

"Whoever exalts himself will be humbled, and whoever humbles himself will be exalted."

Matthew 23:12, NIV

But "he who glories, let him glory in the Lord." For not he who commends himself is approved, but whom the Lord commends.

2 Corinthians 10:17-18, NKJV

Let another man praise thee, and not thine own mouth; a stranger, and not thine own lips.

Proverbs 27:2, KJV

Humble yourselves before the Lord, and he will lift you up.

James 4:10, NIV

"Assuredly, I say to you, unless you are converted and become as little children, you will by no means enter the kingdom of heaven. Therefore whoever humbles himself as this little child is the greatest in the kingdom of heaven."

Matthew 18:3-4, NKJV

But the meek shall inherit the earth; and shall delight themselves in the abundance of peace.

Psalm 37:11, KJV

For the LORD takes delight in his people; he crowns the humble with salvation.

Psalm 149:4, NIV

The meek shall obtain fresh joy in the LORD, and the poor among mankind shall exult in the Holy One of Israel.

Isaiah 29:19, ESV

$\mathcal{I}$DENTITY

To all who did receive him, who believed in his name,
he gave the right to become children of God.

John 1:12, ESV

It should be the goal of every Christian to build his life on the pattern of Christ's life. Of course, it is impossible to reach this goal through your efforts. Trying to do this in your own strength will only lead to frustration and disappointment. When you accept Christ as the Lord of your life, He becomes a reality to you. When you are united with Him, your faith starts to come alive and your whole life is submitted to Him in obedience.

From these dynamics and obedience, a Christlike character develops. The amazing truth is that the person who possesses a character like this is himself not aware of it. There is no false pride. People who are conformed to Christ are too busy loving their fellowmen. They don't have time to try and impress others. Their holiness is a by-product of their fellowship with their Master.

Identity
in God

But thou art he that took me out of the womb: thou didst make me hope when I was upon my mother's breasts. I was cast upon thee from the womb: thou art my God from my mother's belly.

Psalm 22:9-10, KJV

He chose us in him before the creation of the world to be holy and blameless in his sight. In love he predestined us to be adopted as his sons through Jesus Christ.

Ephesians 1:4-5, NIV

For thou art an holy people unto the LORD thy God: the LORD thy God hath chosen thee to be a special people unto himself, above all people that are upon the face of the earth.

Deuteronomy 7:6, KJV

If anyone is in Christ, he is a new creation; old things have passed away; behold, all things have become new.

2 Corinthians 5:17, NKJV

"For whosoever shall do the will of God, the same is my brother, and my sister, and mother."

Mark 3:35, KJV

For in Christ Jesus you are all sons of God, through faith. For as many of you as were baptized into Christ have put on Christ. There is neither Jew nor Greek, there is neither slave nor free, there is neither male nor female, for you are all one in Christ Jesus. And if you are Christ's, then you are Abraham's offspring, heirs according to promise.

Galatians 3:26-29, ESV

You are the temple of the living God. As God has said: "I will dwell in them and walk among them. I will be their God, and they shall be My people." Therefore: "Come out from among them and be separate, says the Lord. Do not touch what is unclean, and I will receive you." "I will be a Father to you, and you shall be My sons and daughters, says the Lord Almighty."

2 Corinthians 6:16-18, NKJV

For all who are led by the Spirit of God are sons of God.

Romans 8:14, ESV

So then you are no longer strangers and aliens, but you are fellow citizens with the saints and members of the household of God, built on the foundation of the apostles and prophets, Christ Jesus himself being the cornerstone, in whom the whole structure, being joined together, grows into a holy temple in the Lord. In him you also are being built together into a dwelling place for God by the Spirit.

Ephesians 2:19-22, ESV

Our fellowship is with the Father and with His Son Jesus Christ.

1 John 1:3, NKJV

And because you are sons, God has sent the Spirit of his Son into our hearts, crying, "Abba! Father!" So you are no longer a slave, but a son, and if a son, then an heir through God.

Galatians 4:6-7, ESV

OY

I will rejoice in the LORD, I will be joyful in God my Savior.

Habakkuk 3:18, NIV

Let us enter each day with joy in our hearts. Let us share the glory of this joy with everyone who crosses our path today. If your faith in Christ is making you a happier person, you will not be able to keep the joy to yourself. Sharing joy with others is a special privilege. An expression of appreciation; a word of encouragement; time spent with someone going through a trial – all these are ways to bring a little light and joy into the lives of others. He who brings sunshine into the lives of others cannot keep the light of that joy from filling his own life.

Happiness and joy come from deep within your heart. They are gifts from God and a fruit of His Spirit. God is, after all, the Source of all true and lasting happiness.

JOY FROM
THE WORD

Rejoice insofar as you share Christ's sufferings, that you may also rejoice and be glad when his glory is revealed.

1 Peter 4:13, ESV

Rejoice in the LORD always. Again I will say, rejoice!

Philippians 4:4, NKJV

Be glad in the LORD, and rejoice, ye righteous: and shout for joy, all ye that are upright in heart.

Psalm 32:11, KJV

We also rejoice in God through our Lord Jesus Christ, through whom we have now received the reconciliation.

Romans 5:11, NKJV

Now the God of hope fill you with all joy and peace in believing, that ye may abound in hope, through the power of the Holy Ghost.

Romans 15:13, KJV

The fruit of the Spirit is love, joy, peace, longsuffering, kindness, goodness, faithfulness, gentleness, self-control.

Galatians 5:22-23, NKJV

"Blessed are you when people insult you, persecute you and falsely say all kinds of evil against you because of me. Rejoice and be glad, because great is your reward in heaven."

Matthew 5:11-12, NIV

When they had called the apostles, and beaten them, they commanded that they should not speak in the name of Jesus, and let them go. And they departed from the presence of the council, rejoicing that they were counted worthy to suffer shame for his name.

Acts 5:40-41, KJV

Therefore with joy shall ye draw water out of the wells of salvation.

Isaiah 12:3, KJV

Surely you have granted him eternal blessings and made him glad with the joy of your presence.

Psalm 21:6, NIV

But let all those rejoice who put their trust in You; let them ever shout for joy, because You defend them; let those also who love Your name be joyful in You. For You, O LORD, will bless the righteous; with favor You will surround him as with a shield.

Psalm 5:11-12, NKJV

The hope of the righteous brings joy, but the expectation of the wicked will perish.

Proverbs 10:28, ESV

"These things I have spoken to you, that My joy may remain in you, and that your joy may be full."

John 15:11, NKJV

That the trial of your faith, being much more precious than of gold that perisheth, though it be tried with fire, might be found unto praise and honour and glory at the appearing of Jesus Christ: Whom having not seen, ye love; in whom, though now ye see him not, yet believing, ye rejoice with joy unspeakable and full of glory.

1 Peter 1:7-8, KJV

$\mathcal{L}$OVE

"A new commandment I give to you, that you love one another; as I have loved you, that you also love one another. By this all will know that you are My disciples, if you have love for one another."

John 13:34-35, NKJV

It was no exaggeration when Paul wrote that if he had gifts of eloquence, prophecy and knowledge and yet was lacking love, all the other gifts went for nothing. Divine love shed abroad in the heart is of all gifts the one that most eloquently interprets and understands the Divine Mind. Before this, prejudices dissolve and barriers fall.

We must, therefore, live our lives in love, under the sweet restraint of God's active love for others. This will please God and make possible a continuance of Christ's own personal ministry to His disciples, as though He again washes their feet, and listens to their triumphs and failures. Let us therefore ask God for a loving spirit that is kind and generous in its judgments, warm in its appreciations, and let us ask that it may be genuine and active.

Promises of
God's love

I the LORD your God am a jealous God, visiting the iniquity of the fathers on the children to the third and the fourth generation of those who hate me, but showing steadfast love to thousands of those who love me and keep my commandments.

Exodus 20:5-6, ESV

Let us love one another, for love comes from God. Everyone who loves has been born of God and knows God. Whoever does not love does not know God, because God is love. No one has ever seen God; but if we love one another, God lives in us and his love is made complete in us.

1 John 4:7-8, 12, NIV

"But love ye your enemies, and do good, and lend, hoping for nothing again; and your reward shall be great, and ye shall be the children of the Highest: for he is kind unto the unthankful and to the evil."

Luke 6:35, KJV

Yet the LORD will command his lovingkindness in the daytime, and in the night his song shall be with me, and my prayer unto the God of my life.

Psalm 42:8, KJV

And above all these put on love, which binds everything together in perfect harmony.

Colossians 3:14, ESV

This is love: not that we loved God, but that he loved us and sent his Son as an atoning sacrifice for our sins. Dear friends, since God so loved us, we also ought to love one another.

1 John 4:10-11, NIV

For I am sure that neither death nor life, nor angels nor rulers, nor things present nor things to come, nor powers, nor height nor depth, nor anything else in all creation, will be able to separate us from the love of God in Christ Jesus our Lord.

Romans 8:38-39, ESV

The love of God has been poured out in our hearts by the Holy Spirit who was given to us.

Romans 5:5, NKJV

Since you have purified your souls in obeying the truth through the Spirit in sincere love of the brethren, love one another fervently with a pure heart.

1 Peter 1:22, NKJV

Your steadfast love, O LORD, extends to the heavens, your faithfulness to the clouds.

Psalm 36:5, ESV

I pray that you, being rooted and established in love, may have power, together with all the saints, to grasp how wide and long and high and deep is the love of Christ, and to know this love that surpasses knowledge – that you may be filled to the measure of all the fullness of God.

Ephesians 3:17-19, NIV

"For God so loved the world, that he gave his only begotten Son, that whosoever believeth in him should not perish, but have everlasting life."

John 3:16, KJV

Above all, keep loving one another earnestly, since love covers a multitude of sins.

1 Peter 4:8, ESV

*L*ONELINESS

"I am with you always, even to the end of the age."
Matthew 28:20, NKJV

Christians need not fear the future, because they are people who live with hope in their hearts, people who are sure that God loves them, people who have guarantees for the way ahead. God sent Jesus to the world precisely because He wants to give His children hope and wants to assure them of His immutable love for them.

Your faith does not prevent storms from coming into your life. But God can guarantee you peace and calm in the midst of the storms of life.

If you belong to God, nothing and no one can ever separate you from His love. God holds you in His hands, and He will carry you when you are no longer able to walk. What's more, He will also help you to carry others and to share His love with them. You can feel God's hands around you in the hands of other believers reaching out to you. *You* can be God's hands by reaching out to others in their times of need.

GOD'S LOVE FOR

THE LONELY

Who shall separate us from the love of Christ? Shall trouble or hardship or persecution or famine or nakedness or danger or sword? No, in all these things we are more than conquerors through him who loved us. For I am convinced that neither death nor life, neither angels nor demons, neither the present nor the future, nor any powers, neither height nor depth, nor anything else in all creation, will be able to separate us from the love of God that is in Christ Jesus our Lord.

Romans 8:35, 37-39, NIV

The LORD is near to all who call on him, to all who call on him in truth.

Psalm 145:18, ESV

Then shalt thou call, and the LORD shall answer; thou shalt cry, and he shall say, Here I am.

Isaiah 58:9, KJV

Where shall I go from your Spirit? Or where shall I flee from your presence? If I ascend to heaven, you are there! If I make my bed in Sheol, you are there! If I take the wings of the morning and dwell in the uttermost parts of the sea, even there your hand shall lead me, and your right hand shall hold me. Even the darkness is not dark to you; the night is bright as the day, for darkness is as light with you.

Psalm 139:7-10, 12, ESV

But if we walk in the light, as he is in the light, we have fellowship with one another.

1 John 1:7, NIV

I have called you by your name; You are Mine. When you pass through the waters, I will be with you; and through the rivers, they shall not overflow you.

Isaiah 43:1-2, NKJV

For He Himself has said, "I will never leave you nor forsake you."

Hebrews 13:5, NKJV

"I will not leave you as orphans; I will come to you."

John 14:18, ESV

And, behold, I am with thee, and will keep thee in all places whither thou goest, ... for I will not leave thee, until I have done that which I have spoken to thee of.

Genesis 28:15, KJV

Look on my right hand and see, For there is no one who acknowledges me; Refuge has failed me; No one cares for my soul. I cried out to You, O Lord: I said, "You are my refuge, My portion in the land of the living."

Psalm 142:4-5, NKJV

A father of the fatherless, and a judge of the widows, is God in his holy habitation. God setteth the solitary in families.

Psalm 68:5-6, NKJV

Nevertheless, I am continually with you; you hold my right hand. You guide me with your counsel, and afterward you will receive me to glory. Whom have I in heaven but you? And there is nothing on earth that I desire besides you. My flesh and my heart may fail, but God is the strength of my heart and my portion forever.

Psalm 73:23-26, ESV

*P*ATIENCE

Be completely humble and gentle; be patient, bearing with one another in love.

Ephesians 4:2, NIV

There are many occasions when we are approached for some advice, support or companionship, and so often we respond only by showing our impatience. We are pressed for time; we have very busy schedules; we are working to beat the clock. We show it in the hurried way in which we try to get rid of people in distress, so that we can rush on to whatever is demanding our attention. This leaves the other person feeling that he is nothing more than an annoying intruder who has to be pushed aside.

If you are faithful to your calling as a follower of Jesus, you should never show impatience or irritation when you are dealing with the distress of other people. Despite your busy life, Christ will always give you the time to do His work. Trust Him unconditionally and you too will be able to treat people with the same patience, compassion and empathy that He did.

THE REWARD

FOR PATIENCE

Rejoice in hope, be patient in tribulation, be constant in prayer.

Romans 12:12, ESV

Now we exhort you, brethren, warn them that are unruly, comfort the feebleminded, support the weak, be patient toward all men.

1 Thessalonians 5:14, KJV

Be patient therefore, brethren, unto the coming of the Lord. Behold, the husbandman waiteth for the precious fruit of the earth, and hath long patience for it, until he receive the early and latter rain. Be ye also patient; stablish your hearts: for the coming of the Lord draweth nigh.

James 5:7-8, KJV

Whatever things were written before were written for our learning, that we through the patience and comfort of the Scriptures might have hope. Now may the God of patience and comfort grant you to be like-minded toward one another.

Romans 15:4-5, NKJV

A man's wisdom gives him patience; it is to his glory to overlook an offense.

Proverbs 19:11, NIV

If we hope for what we do not yet have, we wait for it patiently.

Romans 8:25, NIV

We pray this in order that you may live a life worthy of the Lord and may please him in every way: bearing fruit in every good work, growing in the knowledge of God, being strengthened with all power according to his glorious might so that you may have great endurance and patience.

Colossians 1:10-11, NIV

Take, my brethren, the prophets, who have spoken in the name of the Lord, for an example of suffering affliction, and of patience.

James 5:10, KJV

It is good that one should hope and wait quietly for the salvation of the LORD.

Lamentations 3:26, NKJV

My brethren, count it all joy when ye fall into divers temptations; Knowing this, that the trying of your faith worketh patience. But let patience have her perfect work, that ye may be perfect and entire, wanting nothing.

James 1:2-4, KJV

Wait for the LORD; be strong, and let your heart take courage; wait for the LORD!

Psalm 27:14, ESV

Better a patient man than a warrior, a man who controls his temper than one who takes a city.

Proverbs 16:32, NIV

The Lord is not slow to fulfill his promise as some count slowness, but is patient toward you, not wishing that any should perish, but that all should reach repentance.

2 Peter 3:9, ESV

And let us not grow weary while doing good, for in due season we shall reap if we do not lose heart.

Galatians 6:9, NKJV

$\mathcal{P}$EACE

Since we have been justified through faith, we have
peace with God through our Lord Jesus Christ.

Romans 5:1, NIV

Christ is our peace! He made peace with
God on our behalf. He makes "old" resentful
people into "new" peaceable ones. It is this
peace that enables us to live peacefully with
our fellowmen. We become messengers of
peace as we involve ourselves in activites
that promote peace.

This peace permeates families bringing
joy and harmony because of its influence on
family members. It creates spiritual unity
and togetherness that leads to peace under
the guidance of God. Peace grows in us as
one of the fruits of the Holy Spirit.

All this leads to peace in our souls, because
we are now "all right" in our hearts. All that
was wrong has been removed and Christ is
now the center of our lives. Thus we have a
foretaste of heavenly peace and joy - peace
with God, because our peace depends on
our relationship with God.

Promises

of peace

The LORD bless thee, and keep thee: The LORD make his face shine upon thee, and be gracious unto thee: The LORD lift up his countenance upon thee, and give thee peace.

Numbers 6:24-26, KJV

For to us a child is born, to us a son is given; and the government shall be upon his shoulder, and his name shall be called Wonderful Counselor, Mighty God, Everlasting Father, Prince of Peace. Of the increase of his government and of peace there will be no end, on the throne of David and over his kingdom, to establish it and to uphold it with justice and with righteousness from this time forth and forevermore. The zeal of the LORD of hosts will do this.

Isaiah 9:6-7, ESV

For He Himself is our peace, who has made both one. And He came and preached peace to you who were afar off and to those who were near. For through Him we both have access by one Spirit to the Father.

Ephesians 2:14, 17-18, NKJV

"Peace I leave with you; my peace I give you."

John 14:27, NIV

The mind of sinful man is death, but the mind controlled by the Spirit is life and peace.

Romans 8:6, NIV

Thou wilt keep him in perfect peace, whose mind is stayed on thee: because he trusteth in thee.

Isaiah 26:3, KJV

And the peace of God, which surpasses all understanding, will guard your hearts and your minds in Christ Jesus.

Philippians 4:7, ESV

Let the peace of Christ rule in your hearts, since as members of one body you were called to peace.

Colossians 3:15, NIV

Deceit is in the heart of them that imagine evil: but to the counsellors of peace is joy.

Proverbs 12:20, KJV

The fruit of righteousness is sown in peace by those who make peace.

James 3:18, NKJV

And the effect of righteousness will be peace, and the result of righteousness, quietness and trust forever. My people will abide in a peaceful habitation, in secure dwellings, and in quiet resting places.

Isaiah 32:17-18, ESV

Mark the perfect man, and behold the upright: for the end of that man is peace.

Psalm 37:37, KJV

May the God of peace, who through the blood of the eternal covenant brought back from the dead our Lord Jesus, that great Shepherd of the sheep, equip you with everything good for doing his will.

Hebrews 13:20-21, NIV

"Blessed are the peacemakers: for they shall be called the children of God."

Matthew 5:9, KJV

May the Lord of peace himself give you peace at all times in every way.

2 Thessalonians 3:16, ESV

$\mathcal{P}$ERSEVERANCE

But the one who endures to the end will be saved.
Matthew 24:13, ESV

Perseverance, persistance, courage – these are anchors that we should cling to during the storms of life. Even in the worst storm God has supplied a lifebelt: Faith. The tenacity of your spirit enables you to hold on to that lifebelt.

If you are looking for something to help in the circumstances that are threatening to overwhelm you, then my advice is the same as I would give a drowning person: don't struggle or squirm or fight against the waves in your own strength. Lay your life quietly in God's omnipotent, saving hands. Then you will find peace in the storm and peace creates the power that gives you courage and the ability to persevere. Perseverence is strong but calm. It is courage without bitterness, persistence without self-pity.

As we gradually learn to accept our circumstances rather than rebel against them, we discover a new strength within ourselves.

Promises for

those who persevere

Let us throw off everything that hinders and the sin that so easily entangles, and let us run with perseverance the race marked out for us.

Hebrews 12:1, NIV

Therefore, my beloved brethren, be ye stedfast, unmovable, always abounding in the work of the Lord, forasmuch as ye know that your labour is not in vain in the Lord.

1 Corinthians 15:58, KJV

For we share in Christ, if indeed we hold our original confidence firm to the end.

Hebrews 3:14, ESV

And let us not grow weary of doing good, for in due season we will reap, if we do not give up.

Galatians 6:9, ESV

We also glory in tribulations, knowing that tribulation produces perseverance; and perseverance, character; and character, hope.

Romans 5:3-4, NKJV

Therefore, brethren, stand fast, and hold the traditions which ye have been taught, whether by word, or our epistle.

2 Thessalonians 2:15, KJV

For you have need of endurance, so that when you have done the will of God you may receive what is promised.

Hebrews 10:36, ESV

Behold, we count them happy which endure. Ye have heard of the patience of Job, and have seen the end of the Lord; that the Lord is very pitiful, and of tender mercy.

James 5:11, KJV

You do not lack any spiritual gift as you eagerly wait for our Lord Jesus Christ to be revealed. He will keep you strong to the end, so that you will be blameless on the day of our Lord Jesus Christ.

1 Corinthians 1:7-8, NIV

"Be strong and do not let your hands be weak, for your work shall be rewarded!"

2 Chronicles 15:7, NKJV

"Because you have kept my word about patient endurance, I will keep you from the hour of trial that is coming on the whole world, to try those who dwell on the earth."

Revelation 3:10, ESV

"He that overcometh shall inherit all things; and I will be his God, and he shall be my son."

Revelation 21:7, KJV

If we endure, We shall also reign with Him. If we deny Him, He also will deny us. If we are faithless, He remains faithful; He cannot deny Himself.

2 Timothy 2:12-13, NKJV

The LORD will fulfill his purpose for me; your steadfast love, O LORD, endures forever. Do not forsake the work of your hands.

Psalm 138:8, ESV

"He who stands firm to the end will be saved."

Matthew 24:13, NIV

$\mathcal{P}$RAISE

Exalt the L{\scriptsize ORD} our God; worship at his footstool!
Holy is he!

Psalm 99:5, ESV

It is impossible to clap your hands and sing exultantly to the honor of God and still be gloomy. If you are feeling down-hearted and it seems as if nothing is working out well for you, then start praising and thanking God now. It might sound foolish to you but you can thank God that He is with you in your present situation.

True praise and thanksgiving to the almighty God should not depend on your feelings. When you are down-hearted and depressed, these are the very moments that you need to praise Him. Then you will experience the wonderful, elevating power of praise and thanksgiving. It is the key which God provides you with to open the treasure chambers of life in Him. The simple lifting up of your heart to Him, brings you into His presence and you cannot help but sing His praise and glory.

The Word's view

ON PRAISE

The LORD is my strength and my song, and he has become my salvation; this is my God, and I will praise him, my father's God, and I will exalt him.

Exodus 15:2, ESV

Since we are receiving a kingdom that cannot be shaken, let us be thankful, and so worship God acceptably with reverence and awe.

Hebrews 12:28, NIV

For great is the LORD, and greatly to be praised: he also is to be feared above all gods. Glory and honour are in his presence; strength and gladness are in his place. Give unto the LORD, ye kindreds of the people, give unto the LORD glory and strength. Give unto the LORD the glory due unto his name: bring an offering, and come before him: worship the LORD in the beauty of holiness. Let the heavens be glad, and let the earth rejoice: and let men say among the nations, the LORD reigneth.

1 Chronicles 16:25, 27-29, 31, KJV

I will sing to the LORD as long as I live; I will sing praise to my God while I have my being.

Psalm 104:33, NKJV

O LORD, you are my God; I will exalt you and praise your name, for in perfect faithfulness you have done marvelous things, things planned long ago.

Isaiah 25:1, NIV

Through Jesus, therefore, let us continually offer to God a sacrifice of praise – the fruit of lips that confess his name.

Hebrews 13:15, NIV

I will extol You, my God, O King; And I will bless Your name forever and ever. Every day I will bless You, and I will praise Your name forever and ever. Great is the LORD, and greatly to be praised; and His greatness is unsearchable.

Psalm 145:1-3, NKJV

I will praise the LORD according to his righteousness: and will sing praise to the name of the LORD most high.

Psalm 7:17, KJV

Sing praises to God, sing praises! Sing praises to our King, sing praises! For God is the King of all the earth; sing praises with a Psalm!

Psalm 47:6-7, ESV

Let everything that has breath praise the LORD. Praise the LORD.

Psalm 150:6, NIV

Praise ye the LORD. Sing unto the LORD a new song, and his praise in the congregation of saints. Let Israel rejoice in him that made him: let the children of Zion be joyful in their King. Let them praise his name in the dance: let them sing praises unto him with the timbrel and harp.

Psalm 149:1-3, KJV

Praise the LORD from the heavens; Praise Him in the heights! Praise Him, all His angels; Praise Him, all His hosts! Praise Him, sun and moon; Praise Him, all you stars of light! Praise Him, you heavens of heavens, And you waters above the heavens! Let them praise the name of the LORD, For He commanded and they were created. He also established them forever and ever; He made a decree which shall not pass away.

Psalm 148:1-6, NKJV

$\mathcal{P}$RAYER

Seek the LORD while He may be found, call upon Him while He is near.

Isaiah 55:6, NKJV

Nobody can grow spiritually without a continually developing prayer life. The Master illustrated to us the importance of time alone with God. The same requirement is valid for His modern day disciples if they wish to develop into spiritual maturity. Their faith can only be effective if they have a pulsating prayer life.

Too often prayer is the step-child of spiritual growth instead of being its foundation. It requires strict discipline and regular practice. Don't think your prayers are effective only when you are in the mood to pray. It is often when you don't feel like praying at all that you should persevere.

Make sure that all your prayers are focused on God. Many prayers seem to accentuate problems, instead of praising God for His ability to deal with them.

The Word's view

ON PRAYER

This is the confidence we have in approaching God: that if we ask anything according to his will, he hears us. And if we know that he hears us – whatever we ask – we know that we have what we asked of him.

1 John 5:14-15, NIV

To you, O LORD, I call; my rock, be not deaf to me. Hear the voice of my pleas for mercy, when I cry to you for help, when I lift up my hands toward your most holy sanctuary.

Psalm 28:1-2, ESV

Hear me when I call, O God of my righteousness: thou hast enlarged me when I was in distress; have mercy upon me, and hear my prayer.

Psalm 4:1, KJV

"I say to you: Ask and it will be given to you; seek and you will find; knock and the door will be opened to you. For everyone who asks receives; he who seeks finds; and to him who knocks, the door will be opened."

Luke 11:9-10, NIV

For the eyes of the Lord are on the righteous, and His ears are open to their prayers.

1 Peter 3:12, NKJV

The prayer of a righteous man is powerful and effective.

James 5:16, NIV

Evening and morning and at noon I utter my complaint and moan, and he hears my voice.

Psalm 55:17, ESV

"Therefore I tell you, whatever you ask in prayer, believe that you have received it, and it will be yours."

Mark 11:24, ESV

Give ear, O Lord, to my prayer; and attend to the voice of my supplications. In the day of my trouble I will call upon You, for You will answer me.

Psalm 86:6-7, NKJV

"Whatever you ask in my name, this I will do, that the Father may be glorified in the Son. If you ask me anything in my name, I will do it."

John 14:13-14, ESV

Then you shall call, and the LORD will answer;
you shall cry, and he will say, "Here I am."

Isaiah 58:9, ESV

But certainly God has heard me; He has
attended to the voice of my prayer. Blessed
be God, who has not turned away my prayer,
nor His mercy from me!

Psalm 66:19-20, NKJV

The LORD is far from the wicked: but he
heareth the prayer of the righteous.

Proverbs 15:29, KJV

"But when you pray, go into your room and
shut the door and pray to your Father who
is in secret. And your Father who sees in
secret will reward you."

Matthew 6:6, ESV

"And all things, whatsoever ye shall ask in
prayer, believing, ye shall receive."

Matthew 21:22, KJV

He will surely be gracious to you at the
sound of your cry. As soon as he hears it,
he answers you.

Isaiah 30:19, ESV

SIN AND REPENTANCE

If we confess our sins, He is faithful and just to forgive us our sins and to cleanse us from all unrighteousness.

1 *John* 1:9, NKJV

Grieving about our sins includes many things: anxiety about our betrayal of the living God; our shallowness, disobedience and unwillingness to serve Him; our lack of holiness; our refusal to subject ourselves to His holy will; our devotedness to our worldly possessions, and much more.

However, when Christ speaks of comfort, that judgment places us in the midst of the Gospel of Grace. Our sole comfort in life and in death is that we belong to Jesus our Savior. Christ is the Comfort for all who have learned through grace to grieve about their sins and who know that, through repentance and remission of sins, they belong to Him.

On the cross He carried *our* sins in His body. On this tree He fully becomes our Comforter, Savior and Redeemer. Therefore we rejoice.

THE WORD'S VIEW

ON SIN AND REPENTANCE

"Therefore I will judge you, O house of Israel, every one according to his ways, declares the LORD. Repent and turn from all your transgressions, lest iniquity be your ruin. Cast away from you all the transgressions that you have committed, and make yourselves a new heart and a new spirit!"

Ezekiel 18:30-31, ESV

All have sinned and fall short of the glory of God, and are justified freely by his grace through the redemption that came by Christ Jesus.

Romans 3:23-24, NIV

Remember therefore from where you have fallen; repent, and do the works you did at first. If not, I will come to you and remove your lampstand from its place, unless you repent.

Revelation 2:5, ESV

"The kingdom of God is near. Repent and believe the good news!"

Mark 1:15, NIV

Turn unto the LORD your God: for he is gracious and merciful, slow to anger, and of great kindness, and repenteth him of the evil.

Joel 2:13, KJV

If a wicked man turns from all his sins which he has committed, keeps all My statutes, and does what is lawful and right, he shall surely live; he shall not die. None of the transgressions which he has committed shall be remembered against him.

Ezekiel 18:21-22, NKJV

The Lord is not slack concerning His promise, as some count slackness, but is longsuffering toward us, not willing that any should perish but that all should come to repentance.

2 Peter 3:9, NKJV

Repent, and be baptized every one of you in the name of Jesus Christ for the remission of sins, and ye shall receive the gift of the Holy Ghost.

Acts 2:38, KJV

The LORD is near to the brokenhearted and saves the crushed in spirit.

Psalm 34:18, ESV

"Repent, for the kingdom of heaven is near."

Matthew 3:2, NIV

Let it be known to you therefore, brothers, that through this man forgiveness of sins is proclaimed to you, and by him everyone who believes is freed from everything.

Acts 13:38, ESV

But if we walk in the light, as he is in the light, we have fellowship one with another, and the blood of Jesus Christ his Son cleanseth us from all sin.

1 John 1:7, KJV

"Just so, I tell you, there will be more joy in heaven over one sinner who repents than over ninety-nine righteous persons who need no repentance."

Luke 15:7, ESV

He himself bore our sins in his body on the tree, so that we might die to sins and live for righteousness; by his wounds you have been healed. For you were like sheep going astray, but now you have returned to the Shepherd and Overseer of your souls.

1 Peter 2:24-25, NIV

STRESS

He gives strength to the weary and increases the power of the weak.

Isaiah 40:29, NIV

Stress is the extra demand made on your body during tense or dangerous situations. Your automatic nervous system releases hormones into your blood stream that cause chemical changes. Your heart beats faster, your breathing speeds up, and blood surges to your brain. This causes people either to try to fight the danger, or flee from it.

How can we find peace in times of continuous stress? We need to be aware of our own limitations and strengths. Identify those things that increase stress: feelings of guilt, bitterness, anger, disappointment. Do not carry the burden of the past with you. Don't nurture your grievances. Accept God's forgiveness of you, and forgive yourself.

Learn to relax through friendships, sport, poetry, music, art, the beauties of nature. Work on your relationship with the living Christ. He gives you the grace and peace that you need to handle stress.

Coping

WITH STRESS

Though I walk in the midst of trouble, you preserve my life; you stretch out your hand against the wrath of my enemies, and your right hand delivers me.

Psalm 138:7, ESV

"Come unto me, all ye that labour and are heavy laden, and I will give you rest. Take my yoke upon you, and learn of me; for I am meek and lowly in heart: and ye shall find rest unto your souls. For my yoke is easy, and my burden is light."

Matthew 11:28-30, KJV

Be still, and know that I am God; I will be exalted among the nations, I will be exalted in the earth! The LORD of hosts is with us; the God of Jacob is our refuge.

Psalm 46:10-11, NKJV

Humble yourselves under the mighty hand of God, that He may exalt you in due time, casting all your care upon Him, for He cares for you.

1 Peter 5:6-7, NKJV

Then they cry unto the LORD in their trouble, and he bringeth them out of their distresses. He maketh the storm a calm, so that the waves thereof are still. Then are they glad because they be quiet; so he bringeth them unto their desired haven.

Psalm 107:28-30, KJV

Be careful for nothing; but in every thing by prayer and supplication with thanksgiving let your requests be made known unto God. And the peace of God, which passeth all understanding, shall keep your hearts and minds through Christ Jesus.

Philippians 4:6-7, KJV

The LORD is my shepherd; I shall not want. He makes me to lie down in green pastures; He leads me beside the still waters. He restores my soul; He leads me in the paths of righteousness for His name's sake. Yea, though I walk through the valley of the shadow of death, I will fear no evil; for You are with me; Your rod and Your staff, they comfort me.

Psalm 23:1-4, NKJV

We were under great pressure, far beyond our ability to endure, so that we despaired even of life. Indeed, in our hearts we felt the sentence of death. But this happened that we might not rely on ourselves but on God, who raises the dead. He has delivered us from such a deadly peril, and he will deliver us. On him we have set our hope that he will continue to deliver us.

2 Corinthians 1:8-10, NIV

In God I have put my trust; I will not fear. What can flesh do to me?

Psalm 56:4, NKJV

For God did not give us a spirit of timidity, but a spirit of power, of love and of self-discipline.

2 Timothy 1:7, NIV

"Peace I leave with you, My peace I give to you; not as the world gives do I give to you. Let not your heart be troubled, neither let it be afraid."

John 14:27, NKJV

When I said, My foot slippeth; thy mercy, O Lord, held me up.

Psalm 94:18, KJV

$\mathcal{W}$ISDOM

The fear of the LORD is the beginning of wisdom:
and the knowledge of the holy is understanding.

Proverbs 9:10, KJV

In a world that seems to have confused the accumulation of facts and information with education, wisdom is a scarce commodity. One seldom hears of someone being called wise – clever, yes, knowledgeable, yes – but not wise. Wisdom seems to be relegated to the esoteric and reclusive lifestyle of ancient hermits.

Yet the Bible emphasizes wisdom as a crucial quality in the lives of God's people. Wisdom comes from trusting God and walking with Him so that we learn to see life from His perspective. Wisdom cannot be separated from the character of God – from His love, and His holiness, and His goodness. Wisdom is the ability to understand the true nature of things – ourselves and the world, and helps us develop a clear vision of our purpose in the world as followers of Christ. God gladly gives wisdom to those who ask Him for it – His wisdom that helps us to live in His will.

Wisdom from the Word

He changes times and seasons; he removes kings and sets up kings; he gives wisdom to the wise and knowledge to those who have understanding.

Daniel 2:21, ESV

My purpose is that they may be encouraged in heart and united in love, so that they may have the full riches of complete understanding, in order that they may know the mystery of God, namely, Christ, in whom are hidden all the treasures of wisdom and knowledge.

Colossians 2:2-3, NIV

See, I have taught you statutes and rules, as the LORD my God commanded me, that you should do them in the land that you are entering to take possession of it. Keep them and do them, for that will be your wisdom and your understanding in the sight of the peoples, who, when they hear all these statutes, will say, "surely this great nation is a wise and understanding people."

Deuteronomy 4:5-6, ESV

Let the word of Christ dwell in you richly as you teach and admonish one another with all wisdom.

Colossians 3:16, NIV

For the LORD gives wisdom; from his mouth come knowledge and understanding; he stores up sound wisdom for the upright.

Proverbs 2:6-7, ESV

For God giveth to a man that is good in his sight wisdom, and knowledge, and joy.

Ecclesiastes 2:26, KJV

The wisdom that is from above is first pure, then peaceable, gentle, willing to yield, full of mercy and good fruits, without partiality and without hypocrisy.

James 3:17, NKJV

And the spirit of the LORD shall rest upon him, the spirit of wisdom and understanding, the spirit of counsel and might, the spirit of knowledge and of the fear of the LORD.

Isaiah 11:2, KJV

"Behold, the fear of the LORD, that is wisdom, and to depart from evil is understanding."

Job 28:28, NKJV

Oh, the depth of the riches of the wisdom and knowledge of God! How unsearchable his judgments, and his paths beyond tracing out!

Romans 11:33, NIV

When wisdom enters your heart, and knowledge is pleasant to your soul, discretion will preserve you; understanding will keep you, to deliver you from the way of evil.

Proverbs 2:10-12, NKJV

By insolence comes nothing but strife, but with those who take advice is wisdom.

Proverbs 13:10, ESV

I keep asking that the God of our Lord Jesus Christ, the glorious Father, may give you the Spirit of wisdom and revelation, so that you may know him better.

Ephesians 1:17, NIV

If any of you lacks wisdom, let him ask God, who gives generously to all without reproach, and it will be given him.

James 1:5, ESV

$\mathcal{S}$OURCES

The devotions included in this book have been drawn from the following sources:

1. Mitchell, Fred. 1968. *At Break of Day, Marshall.* Morgan and Scott.
2. Murray, Andrew. 2002. *Humility.* Vereeniging: Christian Art Publishers.
3. Ozrovech, Solly. 2002. *Fountains of Blessing.* Vereeniging: Christian Art Publishers.
4. Ozrovech, Solly. 2000. *The Glory of God's Grace.* Vereeniging: Christian Art Publishers.
5. Ozrovech, Solly. 2000. *Intimate Moments with God.* Vereeniging: Christian Art Publishers.
6. Ozrovech, Solly. 2000. *New Beginnings.* Vereeniging: Christian Art Publishers.
7. Ozrovech, Solly. 2002. *The Voice Behind You.* Vereeniging: Christian Art Publishers.
8. Smit, Nina. 1999. *When the Day Breaks.* Vereeniging: Christian Art Publishers.

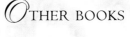

OTHER BOOKS

IN THIS RANGE

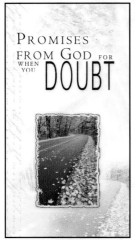

PROMISES FROM GOD FOR WHEN YOU DOUBT

ISBN: 1-86920-072-1

PROMISES FROM GOD FOR WHEN YOU HURT

ISBN: 1-86920-071-3

PROMISES FROM GOD FOR TODAY

ISBN: 1-86920-069-1